THE PRACTICAL GUIDE TO
WORLD-CLASS
IT **SERVICE** MANAGEMENT

THE PRACTICAL GUIDE TO
WORLD-CLASS
IT SERVICE MANAGEMENT

KEVIN J. SMITH

AUTHOR DEDICATION

To Julie: your simple words of
encouragement made everything possible.

For Christopher, Michaela, Zachary, Taylor, Isabella,
and Gianna. Six true miracles. When things get hard,
I close my eyes and think of you.

For Mom and Dad, 58 years and going strong.

For Angi, Chris, and Paul. My brothers and sister.

For Gene Kranz, Bill Gibson, and Michael McCloskey.
Mentors who patiently taught so much.

ACKNOWLEDGMENTS

The birth of a book is only possible through the efforts of many people, each making contributions large and small, every one of which plays a unique and vital role.

My sincere thanks to John Ferron, whose enthusiastic support and sponsorship were instrumental in taking the leap from a very rough idea to reality.

I am fortunate to work with a team of talented business professionals and IT Service Management experts every day, and their input, feedback, review of copy and ideas were instrumental in shaping the content of this book. In particular my thanks go to Vijay Chodavarapu, Greg Clancy, Steve Gardner, Mike Heberling, Mark Hodgen, David Iannotti, Randy Jessee, Robert Kelsall, Josh Ko, Chris Lawton, Vincent Lin, Hipolito Luis, David Martinez, Prajval Parthasarathy, Tony La Rosa, Eddie Lopez, Suresh Pandian, Jason Rose, Darryl Sarkisian, Michael Skinner, Lee Stafford, Alan Taylor, Jennifer Voshake and Gary Wang.

For the past ten years I have had the opportunity and privilege to collaborate with leading IT organizations and

Service Management professionals delivering vital services every day in diverse markets around the world. These organizations include ASCAP, Avis, Circle K, Children's Hospital, Canon, Cleary Gottlieb, Cleveland Clinic, Co-op, Horace Mann, Johnson Matthey, LabCorp, NYU Medical Center, Newell Rubbermaid, Oxford University, Pizza Hut, Randstad Staffing, SCI Corp, SCL Health, Total Wine, Trinity Industries, UNC Health, and CST Brands.

For taking my very rough and often ugly sketches and transforming them into the handsome figures within these pages, a sincere thanks to my illustrator, Julie Felton.

And, to the good people at Outskirts Press, it has been a joy to work with you and my sincere thanks for your patience and encouragement.

FOREWORD

The Help Desk rose from humble beginnings. As our dependence on machines, including personal computers and the ever-confounding printer, grew in the 1970s and 1980s, organizations of virtually every shape and size found they desperately needed help when their machines would inevitably break. The solution was to find a few smart people who knew something about technology and make them available on a desk where workers in every organization could go to get help.

> *A machine would break and the Help Desk*
> *would be ready with a fix.*

Much has changed in the thirty years since, and today, in the ever-changing and wonderful world of IT Service Management, I put pen to paper to offer a readable and usable reference for those who practice this craft and work hard every day to support the organization, its people and its customers. My humble hope is that the dedicated people in IT and any team that provides employee or customer-facing services can find some useful bits of information throughout the book that will find a place in the business every day.

The scope of IT Service Management has grown vastly in the past thirty years, and it was simply not possible to address all the elements that have emerged during that time in a single book and in one that I wanted above all else to be readable and usable. So, I have selected a key set of topics and processes that together provide a useful framework for an organization implementing a new—or improving an existing—IT Service Management function. No single set of processes will work for every organization, so the selections in this book are intended to provide a common set of processes that **will be practical** for most organizations, along with complementary topics that will provide guidance for the successful implementation of these processes.

One such useful topic is the chapter on The Consumerization of IT Service Management

The chapters are designed to stand alone and can be referenced individually or in any combination. My expectation is that only a few very brave souls will read the book from front to back and that most of you will reference specific chapters based on the current state of projects and the needs of the organization. While one company might be focused on Change Management, another will be rolling out Service Catalog for the first time and looking for some guidance on how best to be productive in implementing this transformational process.

With a growing and sometimes overwhelming set of best practices and standards developing across the IT Service Management market today, the content of each chapter is structured to blend the basic elements of proven best practices with real-world experience. As such this is not a book about ITIL; there are many useful references on ITIL for those who need the full structure, scope and detail on ITIL. Similarly, it is not a book about COBIT or ISO. But, because I believe these elements have a place today in IT Service Management, you will find a chapter that provides a brief summary for each of these three standards in order to help you with a basic understanding of each. Then, as we look at each of the six core elements and then the twelve world-class elements of Practical IT Service Management, there will be some components of each incorporated but only to the extent that they are both useful and practical. Note these twelve elements may or may not map clearly to any existing framework, and this is intentional based on what I see companies practicing today and what is truly useful and practical.

At the end of most chapters you will find a section offering Tips for Success.

These tips are relevant to the topic of the chapter and provide a simple reference for key things to remember or key behaviors that can make the difference between success and failure. These tips are based on many experiences with companies in different industries and organizations of all sizes and are intended to be adaptable to a broad range of organizations. I hope you find them useful and they bring some clarity to your ultimate path to success. Not a comprehensive plan, of course, but a pragmatic checklist. I do love lists.

It is not possible to address the practice of IT Service Management without recognizing the evolution of our industry over the past 25 years, beginning with its origins at the birth of Help Desk in the 1980s. The chapter on A Brief History of Service Management will provide an overview of this evolution, and throughout the book you will find references to Help Desk, Service Desk, Service Management and IT Service Management. In many respects these operations are very similar and in others they are very different, but in either case the evolution does provide a helpful context for the current state of Service Management.

> *A Brief History of Service Management shows an overview of the evolution of Help Desk, Service Desk and IT Service Management.*

Because some concepts are best captured with a diagram or graphic, I make extensive use of illustrations throughout the book. As a reader, I find them helpful, and my hope is that these illustrations will help the content to be more useful with the added benefit of making the book a more practical reference and, of course, more readable.

Finally, I encourage you to enjoy the journey of seeking World-Class IT Service Management.

Bring with you a joie de vivre every day
and enjoy the transformation we are in the
midst of today.

This attitude will show and affect everything you and your teammates do every day in delivering world-class service. First comes commitment, and with this commitment to deliver outstanding service to your employees and clients, you will discover ways to improve a little bit every day. Therein lies a remarkable sense of satisfaction and a self-sustaining passion that will unlock limitless value for your organization and business.

TABLE OF CONTENTS

CHAPTER 1

SCOPE OF THE BOOK: THE CORE 6 AND WORLD-CLASS 12

The growth, evolution and emerging elegance of IT Service Management methodologies, standards and best practices can be both a blessing and at times a challenge. The good news is that we have more mature processes and proven methods to provide guidance when setting out to build a new—or improve an existing—Service Desk operation. The not-so-good news is that the volume, scope and detail of these same frameworks and methods can be intimidating, difficult to understand and in some cases simply overwhelming for many in search of simple and practical concepts.

Today, one of our most commonly referenced frameworks is ITIL, and the 2011 update to ITIL defines approximately twenty-seven distinct functions and processes. Based on my experience working with leading organizations and IT

Service Management teams over the past 10+ years, and in order to stay true to the goal of this book providing a practical reference, I have selected twelve elements that in some combination will meet the needs of the high majority of IT Service Management organizations, regardless of size or industry.

These twelve elements are as follows:

1. Incidents
2. Service Requests
3. Problem Management
4. Service Catalog
5. Knowledge Management
6. Service Level Management
7. Asset and Configuration Management
8. Change Management
9. Release Management
10. Availability Management
11. Financial Management
12. Service Portfolios

Note these twelve elements do not necessarily line up verbatim with ITIL or any of the common standards or frameworks.

I have selected this set of twelve because they represent how high-performing organizations both think and work every day.

Virtually every organization can manage services in a world-class way with the right combination of these twelve elements put into action. Every organization is different, and as such there is no single model or prescription that will work for every business.

This is an important point. Simply implementing a process or group of processes does not a great Service Desk make. The implementation of the elements described in these pages simply creates the opportunity to be great and, for some organizations, world-class. But, equally important— and perhaps more important—is the **cultural shift and evolution** that must accompany the operation of these elements.

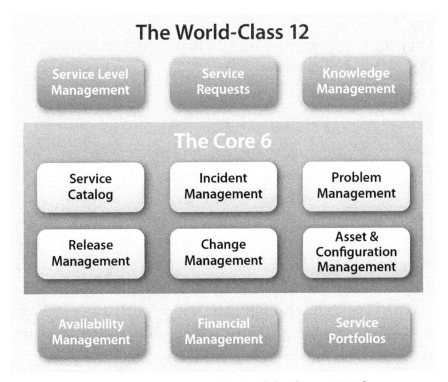

Figure 1.1: The Core 6 and World-Class 12 Elements

In the interest of providing further clarity, I have selected six elements from the larger set of twelve, and we will refer to this group as the **Core 6** processes. Based on what I have seen in working with hundreds of IT Service Management teams, virtually all of them are operating these six core elements/processes in some form:

1. Incidents
2. Problem Management
3. Service Catalog
4. Asset & Configuration Management
5. Change Management
6. Release Management

We can, of course, discuss and debate the makeup of this list.

> *But the Core 6 is always a good model for building a foundation, and in some cases a complete model, for long-term IT Service Management success.*

Note that I dedicated a full chapter to a relatively new process in Service Catalog, and this will be a surprise for some of you. I address this in much more detail in Chapter 6, but Service Catalog has rapidly gained in popularity and earned the praise of many over the past five years as a transformational process that drives value and fundamentally changes the role of IT in the organization.

Don't be fooled by the names—they should not be taken as an absolute. A Service Desk can be world-class, operating the six core processes, while an organization operating all of the world-class 12 can be anything but world-class. It is about much more than the processes.

Incident Management and Self-Service are closely related and in many cases overlapping processes, and as such they are both addressed in Chapter 4. Self-Service is very important and, for many organizations, provides an easy-to-use and cost-effective portal for managing incidents, and in some cases for submitting service requests.

A further clarification worthy of mentioning is the inclusion of the CMDB in the chapter on Asset & Configuration Management. This should not be interpreted as a show of disrespect for the CMDB—it has a vital role in world-class IT Service Management.

However, we can think of the CMDB as somewhat inert on its own, and the real fun begins when the CMDB is leveraged with core processes, including Configuration Management and Change Management.

The best organizations recognize this synergy, and this approach is reflected throughout the structure of the book.

While **Service Automation** is a horizontal element that reaches into many of the other processes, I felt it needed a chapter of its own to adequately capture this dynamic topic and discuss some of the important details of automation that should be understood and leveraged.

Financial Management and Service Portfolios are not normally in scope for the early phases of implementing a world-class IT Service Management model, but as organizations mature they will organically create the opportunity to achieve more financial discipline and accountability along with a more strategic view of the full set of services offered by IT. Expect these two elements to gain much more attention over the next ten years.

Only you can determine if some combination of the Core 6 elements will fulfill your vision of world-class IT Service Management or if you have the resources and organizational commitment to operate the full set of the World-Class 12 processes. There are a very few elite organizations that will operate processes beyond the twelve, but my experience has been that these organizations are rare indeed.

Regardless of the current state of your own evolution, it is important to identify the model that is best for your organization, nothing more and nothing less.

Therein lies the essence of your exciting journey.

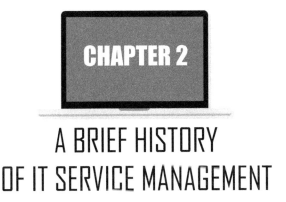

A BRIEF HISTORY
OF IT SERVICE MANAGEMENT

As technology such as phone systems, mini-computers, portable computers, and printers became more useful and more prevalent in virtually all businesses during the '70s and '80s, this technology would inevitably break, which would impact both the individual and the full organization. As a result, the users of this technology would look for help from technology experts to fix these problems and get them back to doing their jobs as quickly as possible.

> *This fundamental collision of technology*
> *and a business need led to the birth of the*
> *Help Desk.*

We begin to see references to the Help Desk in the late '80s but the function had been in its early stages of development for some time. And, of course, we had people doing what they could to help their colleagues before we had a name for what was occurring as a natural evolution. As the needs of business grew and technology continued to find its way into virtually every part of the organization, the first generation of Help Desk software applications appeared, born of this cry for help. The applications facilitated improved processes, faster response times and faster resolution times. Help Desk became an increasingly recognized term, and jobs and roles began to form around this function. By today's standards, the tools were simplistic, but they had a big impact and were widely recognized by the industry.

> *As is often the case, global forces were at work and businesses across the globe struggled with many of the same issues.*

A large IT investment and awareness in the UK gave birth to the Central Communications and Telecommunications Agency (CCTA) in 1986 and the subsequent Government Information Technology Infrastructure Management (GITMM) in 1988. Although not perfectly clear, we can point to these programs as the lineage of the Information Technology Infrastructure Library (ITIL), named as such in 1989 and often traced to 1986 and the formation of CCTA. The first ITIL book, *Service Level Management, Help Desk* along with *Change Management and Contingency Planning* appeared in 1989. In 1990, we saw *Problem Management, Configuration Management, and Cost Management for IT Services* published. Continuing the evolution, the Information Technology Senior Management Forum (ITSMF) was born in 1997.

The birth date of ITIL v2 is a point of some disagreement but generally placed between 1996 and 2000. I have selected the earlier date in recognition of the time these new generations require to take shape and to ultimately be named. Service Support v2 was published in 2000, followed by Service Delivery v2, published in early 2001. CCTA then became part of the Office of Government Commerce (OGC) and Microsoft released the Microsoft Operations Framework (MOF) based on ITIL. *Software Asset Management* was published in 2003 and the ITIL v2 glossary was published in 2006 followed by the five ITIL v3 core books in May 2007.

At a high level we can frame a timeline for the four versions of ITIL as follows:

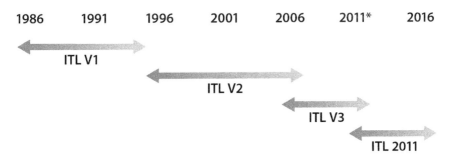

* July 2011, ITIL 2011 Published

Figure 2.1 Overview of ITIL History

Note that the sources we have available don't all agree on the precise dates, but this timeline is close enough for our discussion. On a parallel course with ITIL and through the decade of the '90s, the Help Desk grew in stature as did our dependence on technology and new useful tools including personal computers and the new generation of mobile phones.

We needed the Help Desk more than ever.

The initial focus of the Help Desk was on three core elements: Call Logging, Problem Resolution and Change Management. The purpose of this chapter is to provide an overview of the history and a timeline for Service Management, so we won't attempt to address the details of these processes here.

But it is important to recognize the influence of these humble beginnings on the IT Service Management functions and processes of today.

As the Help Desk developed in businesses during this period, the phone was the primary means of contact, so call management, call handling, and Call Logging were common models for managing the lifecycle of an issue. These original processes evolved into Ticket Management and later Incident Management under ITIL. Chapter 4 explores incidents, and Chapter 5 looks at service requests in much more detail, along with the evolution we have seen from the early ticketing systems.

Although terminology has changed and processes have evolved, the fundamental objective of call handling and call logging was to manage a request or reported issue through a lifecycle resulting in a return to normal operations.

As the grandfather of the modern Service Request and Incident Management processes, the family resemblance is clear.

Problem resolution has been a key element for the Help Desk from the beginning and remains critical today. Problem resolution for the Help Desk was both solving and closing reported issues, and performing an analysis in order to understand and prevent future issues. Over time our focus on proactive prevention has grown and our tools have improved, but again the fundamental objective has changed little.

The third fundamental element of the original Help Desk was Change Management—a strategic process then and now, and a process that has resulted in a significant impact to the business.

The Service Desk

The natural evolution of the Help Desk, including a broader range of services offered, combined with the influences of ITIL and other best practices began to shape the Service Desk and its emergence in the early 2000s. While many organizations continue to refer to a "Help Desk" function, Service Desk has become the more common term, with this shift being traced to approximately 2012. While the Service Desk typically refers to a specific function and a specific team of people in a business or organization, service management is more holistic, touching many elements of the organization and shaping many behaviors, and to a degree executed and operated by the Service Desk.

The fundamental purpose of the Service Desk is to restore normal operations as quickly as possible when an issue is reported and to fulfill service requests.

> *While the basic nature of a call/ticket/incident has changed little in the past twenty-five years...*

we have seen significant changes in the area of service requests. A service request can be many things, including a simple question, ordering a mobile phone, or reserving a conference room for a meeting. Matching the diversity of the service request itself, we have seen a significant growth in the source of service requests beyond the phone. For the first time in history, we are at the threshold of more incidents and service requests originating from non-phone sources like email, self-service portals, and the Service Catalog than those coming from a phone contact.

Changes in business have also shaped the organization and location of the Service Desk. While the original Help Desk was normally local, the Service Desk of today could be local or could be offered through a shared services model which includes a centralized team and function, offering services to multiple and distributed organizations. The Service Desk might also be virtual, leveraging a mobile workforce that can be located anywhere and using mobile devices in combination with the Internet.

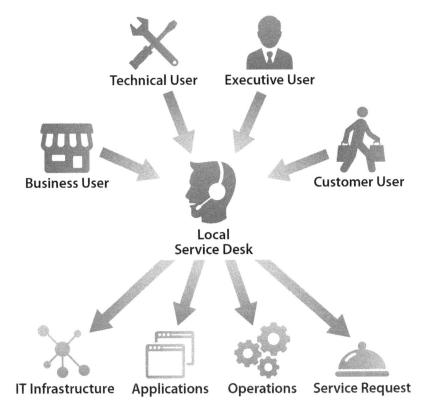

Figure 2.2 The Local Service Desk

The traditional model for Service Desk and the most common model today is the local Service Desk. This model normally consists of a local Service Desk team co-located with the users the desk will provide service to. Service requests may be originated by email, phone, web portal, or walk-up. Due to the location of the Service Desk team, often in the same building as the users, walk-up support is more common and presents its own set of challenges. For the user, a walk-up can be a great experience in that it can result in a quick resolution to the issue and a face-to-face and personal consultation with the analyst. From the standpoint of the

Service Desk, these walk-ups are difficult to plan for and at their worst can be disruptive. A word of caution here:

> *Recall that the ultimate goal of world-class IT Service Management is a happy and productive user whose issue has been resolved and/or request fulfilled.*

Metrics and productivity measures should not cause us to lose sight of this primary objective, and as such, walk-ups should be welcomed. It is important that these items do get logged, as they are sometimes overlooked and can contribute to a less-than-accurate view of the real service and value the desk delivers in a typical day.

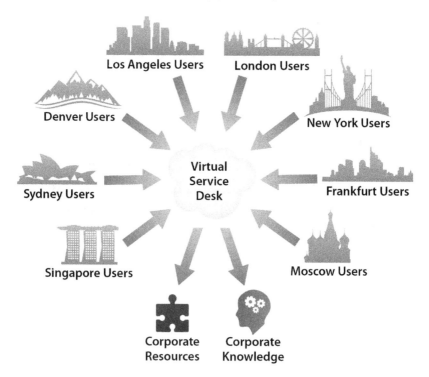

Figure 2.3 The Global Service Desk

Increasingly, business is conducted on a global basis and driven by a distributed workforce. The organization leverages the right people with the right skills regardless of location.

This global and virtual model is now feasible for several reasons:

1. An increase in the number of global centers of commerce.
2. An evolution of the thinking of business leaders—essentially to think and plan globally, then act locally.
3. Improved technology—powerful mobile phones, the Internet, texting and messaging as a preferred and efficient communication method, social media, and much more—allows us to stay connected to our colleagues and customers in a fast and effective way, from anywhere.

A natural extension of this global business model is the global Service Desk. While physically different, the model is logically very much the same as the local Service Desk. In many cases the experience of the user is the same. This is exactly as designed and the benefits of the global Service Desk or virtual Service Desk model appear in the areas of 24x7 support, also commonly referred to by practitioners as a "follow the sun model," the ability to leverage experts on a bigger scale and to realize efficiencies of cost combined with faster service. The best of both worlds when implemented properly.

While the two examples we have shown in Figures 2.2 and

2.3 capture a basic, traditional model and a more complex global model, many organizations will find a model that is **practical**, and somewhere in between.

This could include a combination of a local Service Desk(s) supporting larger numbers of concentrated users, at corporate headquarters, for example, along with strategically located regional Service Desks that support a number of field offices or divisions that span multiple locations and could be multinational if required. Today we are increasingly conducting business on a global scale.

> *This highlights the versatility and flexibility of a healthy Service Desk model—a model that is ultimately driven by great people with a passion for service.*

IT Service Management Today

While IT Service Management has seen many changes over the past thirty years, the heart of the Service Desk remains the same: to deliver great service in a cost-effective and timely manner. The evolution of technology, the emergence of best practices, and the emergence of global markets both support and enhance this primary mission while at the same time creating new challenges.

Change is constant and as such we should expect this to continue for the next thirty years and beyond.

Where there is an organization delivering goods or services to a customer, there will be service management in some form. This need is fundamental and timeless.

In the coming chapters we will take a closer look at special topics that complement IT Service Management and will provide a **practical** model, along with a description of twelve elements that will meet the needs of most organizations striving to deliver world-class IT Service Management.

CHAPTER 3

UNDERSTANDING ITIL, COBIT, AND ISO

If you are reading this book, it is likely that you are not seeing the acronyms of ITIL, COBIT, and ISO for the first time here. Because each of these have a place in IT and in some cases in IT Service Management, I thought it important to provide a high-level summary of each as a bit of helpful context for the book. Each of the following three sections will provide a history, an overview of what it is, including a structure of the framework or standard, and then a description of the relationship between each subject and IT Service Management. If you would like to know more, a good place to start would be with the primary references shown in the back of the book.

ITIL

The origins of ITIL are traced to the 1980s, when challenges with the quality of service delivered to the UK government led to a charter being delivered to the CCTA (Central Computer and Telecommunications Agency) to develop an improved and structured methodology for the delivery of IT services. The CCTA would later become the OGC (Office of Government Commerce) and this work expanded and accelerated as over the next 30 years the challenges originally identified by UK governmental departments were recognized as reflecting a global and consistent need. The original charter has evolved to reflect both internal (employees and customers inside an organization) and external (partners, suppliers, and customers outside the organization) services and the simultaneous evolution of technology. For we Americans who like to believe that all advancements in business and technology in the past seventy-five years have come from the USA and

to settle the many arguments over dinner or a drink regarding who gave us ITIL, it is clearly a gift from our colleagues in the UK.

The good work done by the OGC was ultimately published as the Information Technology Infrastructure Library (ITIL), the name that we continue to use today.

While ITIL can be described in many different ways—and I have heard hundreds of versions over the past ten years—let's keep it simple. I encourage you to think of ITIL as a set of proven best practices that can help IT organizations of all sizes to improve the delivery of services. ITIL provides a structure and a collection of processes that are supported by details that can serve as a useful reference for IT organizations wishing to improve performance today while preparing to meet the challenges of the future.

The latest version of ITIL provides a service lifecycle model as a basis for the evolution of IT Service Management. The service lifecycle as shown by OGC ITIL v3 books is as follows:

Figure 3.1 The Service Lifecycle

This service lifecycle model is intended to provide a flexible and adaptable framework for the continued evolution of ITIL.

It is common in IT organizations today to utilize the ITIL framework as a helpful reference in many respects, including the five primary components of the library as follows:

1. Service Strategy
2. Service Design
3. Service Transition
4. Service Operation
5. Continual Service Improvement

In particular, the processes included with each of these components provide a proven and mature design that can help direct the day-to-day operations and activities of IT and the details necessary to drive the quality of service delivery. These processes and the associated terminology are commonly used in IT organizations around the world today, and we should take a moment to understand where these processes fit in the service lifecycle. I hope this context will help your overall appreciation and understanding of IT Service Management, although certainly

> ***not absolutely necessary to operate a Service Desk, as some companies today, including very successful businesses, are just beginning the journey to world-class IT Service Management***

and have a very limited understanding of ITIL. This is perfectly understandable, as every organization has unique needs and must move forward on a timeline that is shaped to their organization. It is a testament to the value and lasting influence of ITIL that some organizations are just now discovering its contents.

The functions and processes of Service Strategy:

Figure 3.2 ITIL Service Strategy

I explain the scope of this book in Chapter 1 and that it does not align directly with all the processes of ITIL. But I do include Financial Management and Service Portfolio Management among the World-Class 12 processes.

Following Service Strategy is Service Design:

Figure 3.3 Service Design

Of the seven functions and processes offered in Service Design, I have included Service Catalog in the Core 6, and Service Level Management and Availability Management in the group of the World-Class 12.

Next, we look at Service Transition:

Figure 3.4 Service Design

From these additional functions and processes, I have selected Change Management, Service Asset and Configuration Management, Release and Deployment Management for the Core 6, and Knowledge Management for the World-Class 12.

Service Operation follows Service Transition with an additional eight processes and functions:

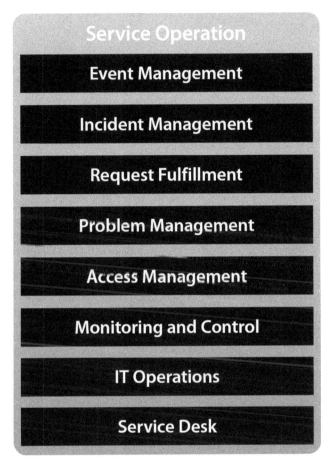

Figure 3.5 Service Operation

From the eight powerful elements of Service Operation, I selected Incident Management and Problem Management for the Core 6 and Request Fulfillment for the World-Class 12.

The final set of ITIL functions and processes belong to Continual Service Improvement:

Figure 3.6 Continual Service Improvement

In taking this pass through the complete set of the five components of ITIL and their processes and functions, you begin to appreciate the full scope of ITIL. It also sheds some light on the magnitude of the undertaking when an organization embarks on the journey of IT Service Management with an aspiration to implement the ITIL framework.

The definitive number of ITIL functions and processes can be debated, and to make matters a bit more complicated, the scope of ITIL continues to evolve. But for the purposes of this discussion, we will work with the number of twenty-seven. For virtually every organization, regardless of size, industry, or business model, if an IT Service Desk is in place and services are delivered internally or externally, some combination of the ITIL processes will provide a good starting model for operating today and into the future. What that model is, of course, is dependent on many factors.

It is important to note, and this point is sometimes lost, that

ITIL is a set of best practices and a flexible framework that is not intended to be adapted to the letter, but rather used as guidance

and adapted to the specific organization—recognizing there are unique considerations that make no two businesses or organizations exactly the same. This is both the beauty and the source of potential confusion inherent in ITIL.

This is also the fundamental point I address in Chapter 1 and why I have called the book *A Practical Guide*. As a closing remark for the section, a visual overview of the five ITIL components can be helpful:

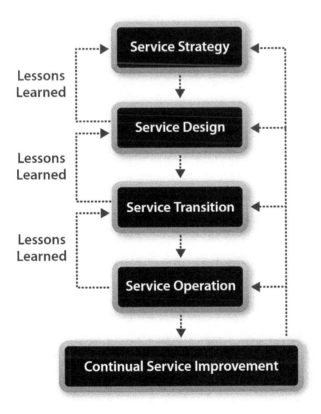

Figure 3.7 ITIL Overview

This simple schematic captures a very important characteristic of ITIL; continuous improvement is a fundamental part of the model, and we will never stop learning and applying our successes and failures back into the business. This mind-set and culture are to be embraced and will help sustain the healthy advancement of each process.

COBIT

Control Objectives for Information and Related Technology (COBIT) was introduced in 1996 and was originally developed to address the needs of auditors focused specifically on technology and controls for technology. COBIT also has a close relationship with Sarbanes-Oxley (SOX) and Sox Section 404 and provided a tool to assist companies with achieving compliance with Sox 404 IT governance. COBIT has proven to be useful to many global enterprises, as it provides detailed guidance for internal controls related to the IT resources inherent to the infrastructure of the modern enterprise.

Although COBIT is best suited to auditors and internal controls, it also provides a valuable reference for IT management and for senior leadership across the enterprise. With the growing complexities and challenges facing today's enterprise, COBIT can help navigate the demands of IT governance and managing the risks inherent to IT assets.

The COBIT framework is formed around five guiding principles.

An Integrated IT Framework: COBIT Principle #1

COBIT emphasizes the importance of aligning IT operations and services with the broader business.

Stakeholder Value Drivers: COBIT Principle #2

IT operating processes should be designed to ensure the delivery of measurable value while optimizing costs throughout the lifecycle of a service or product.

Resources Focus on a Business Context: COBIT Principle #3

All IT technology, information, components, and people should be managed to an optimal level of investment that maximizes the enterprise's leverage of technology and information.

Risk Management: COBIT Principle #4

As stewards of the enterprise and all its assets, the management team must have a complete understanding and awareness of compliance requirements, the current state of risk in the enterprise, and the current and evolving strategy to manage risk to an acceptable level.

Performance Management: COBIT Principle #5

Measurement and reporting processes should be implemented to ensure visibility and understanding of performance factors that directly support the primary goals of IT governance.

With the context of the five COBIT principles, it helps to now look at the process elements of COBIT organized into four process groups:

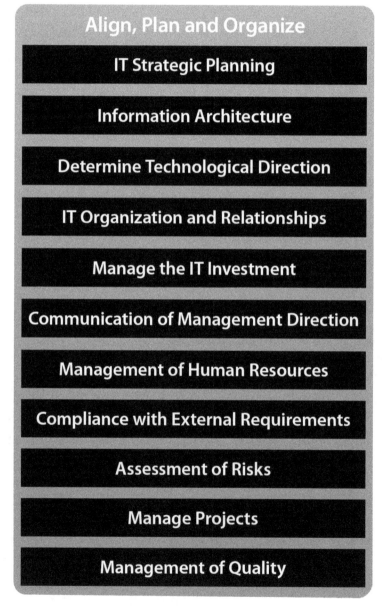

Figure 3.8 COBIT Process Group 1

Our second process group is that of Build, Acquire, and Implement:

Figure 3.9 COBIT Process Group 2

Note the significant differences and a few similarities between the COBIT processes and the twelve ITIL processes we review in the scope of this book.

The third COBIT process group is Deliver, Service, and Support:

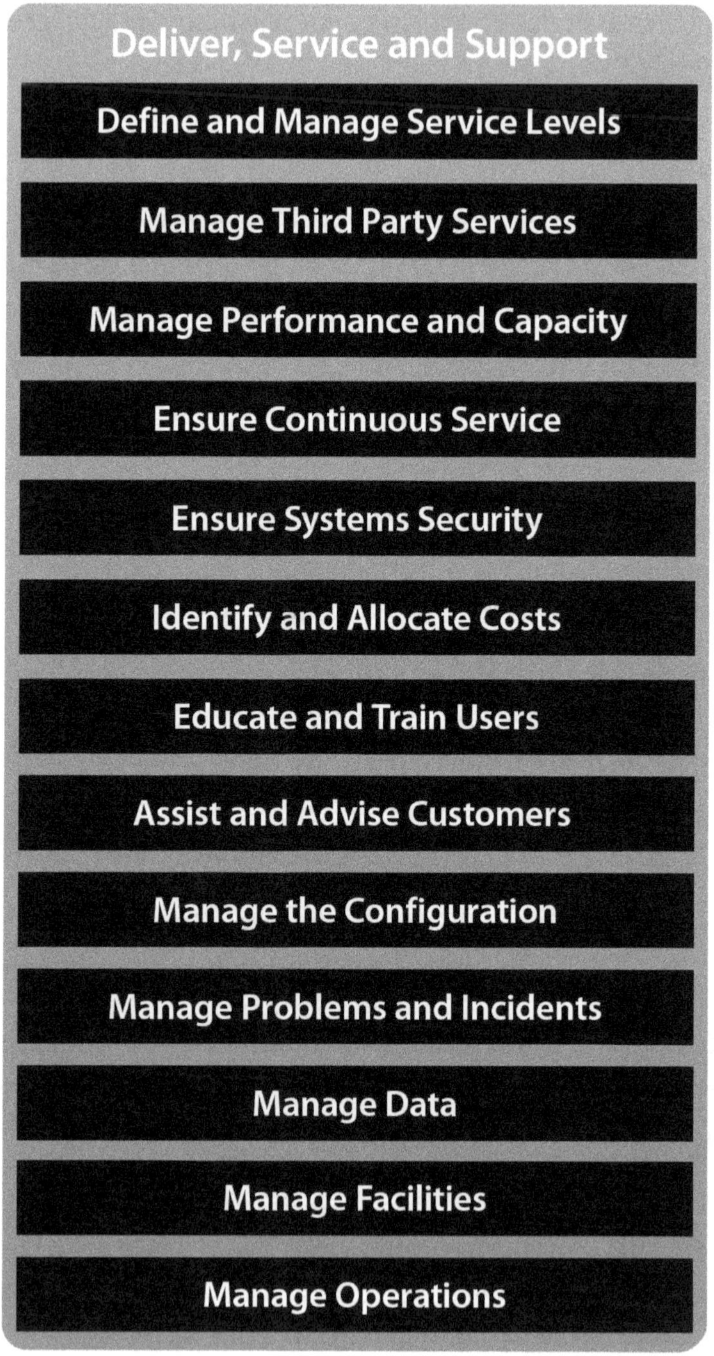

Deliver, Service and Support

- Define and Manage Service Levels
- Manage Third Party Services
- Manage Performance and Capacity
- Ensure Continuous Service
- Ensure Systems Security
- Identify and Allocate Costs
- Educate and Train Users
- Assist and Advise Customers
- Manage the Configuration
- Manage Problems and Incidents
- Manage Data
- Manage Facilities
- Manage Operations

Figure 3.10 COBIT Process Group 3

With this third COBIT process group including Service and Support, note the intersection with the following IT Service Management processes:

1. Incident Management
2. Problem Management
3. Configuration Management
4. Manage Service Levels

And beyond these direct overlaps, other areas have a complementary relationship with IT Service Management and ITIL, including:

1. Continuous Service
2. Assisting Customers
3. Managing Third Parties
4. Managing Capacity
5. Managing Data

This makes more sense when we consider that both ITIL and COBIT are intended to support a broad set of IT goals, albeit with some differences in methods and focus.

The fourth COBIT process group is Evaluate, Direct, and Monitor:

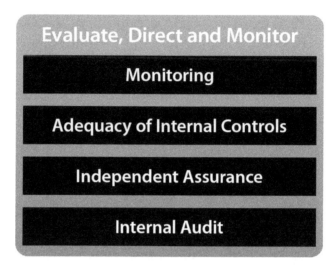

Figure 3.11 COBIT Process Group 4

The COBIT framework can be seen as quite detailed and complex. This detail and complexity can be a strength when used effectively and smartly, and when applied with careful planning to the specific requirements of an enterprise.

> *There is a certain elegance to COBIT that one begins to appreciate after careful study.*

It also becomes clear that COBIT can be useful to a broad range of global enterprises, large and small, in virtually any industry.

However, this chapter is intended to be a simple overview of COBIT, so as much fun as it would be, it's beyond our scope to dive deeper into COBIT for now. One of the key characteristics of COBIT is its multidimensional model that combines principles, objectives, processes, and goals. This design helps to create the flexibility of the COBIT framework. In recognizing this, there is one more part of the model we will look at—the seventeen IT-related goals, each of which can be mapped to the COBIT processes.

To help organize the goals and provide some context for each, COBIT provides four high-level and logical categories:

1. Corporate
2. Customer
3. Internal
4. Learning

These simple categories also say a lot about the focus of each goal. The following tables take each of the seventeen IT-related goals and place them in one of the four categories. This allows us to better triangulate the framework effectively:

Figure 3.12 COBIT Corporate Goals

As the category name implies, this set of goals is focused on establishing a governance framework, cultivating enterprise value, providing shareholder transparency, managing risk, and providing a management methodology for security, continuity, operations, and service requests in combination with incidents.

The second category is focused on the customer.

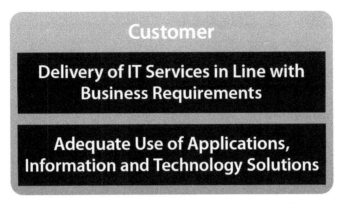

Figure 3.13 COBIT Customer Goals

These goals are intended to address the needs of connecting the performance of the business to the needs of customers. This incorporates business requirements, applications, enterprise information, and technology. This framework can help provide guidance to enterprise IT models including a federated database, enterprise business processes, managing continuity, and creating controls to manage cross-functional business processes.

The third category addresses a broad set of internal goals.

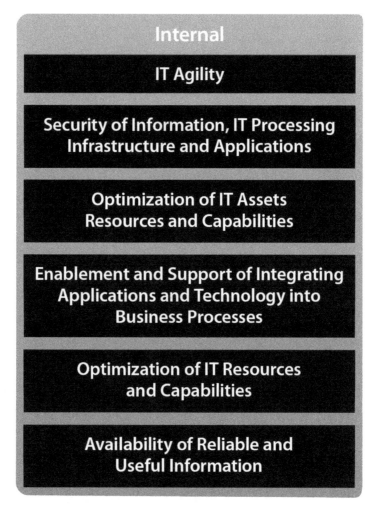

Figure 3.14 COBIT Internal Goals

Key themes and focus areas for the internal goals include optimizing IT resources, ensuring risk optimization, secure and reliable information, policy compliance, managing problems and the risk they pose to the business, and managing the security of IT infrastructure and applications.

The fourth category addresses goals in support of learning.

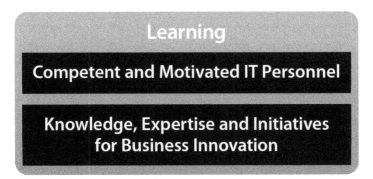

Figure 3.15 COBIT Learning Goals

These are important goals that balance the Corporate, Customer, and Internal goals reviewed in the previous three categories and fifteen goals. The twin goals associated with Learning are building value into the enterprise by investing in a highly skilled and highly motivated workforce.

> *This cultivation of great people will lead to a high-performing business fueled by thought leadership and innovation.*

This then translates into strong market performance and success with customers.

COBIT is a sophisticated and multifaceted framework that can provide a useful and adaptable tool in virtually any enterprise looking to improve internal controls and create a strong and rigorous model for IT governance and the associated processes. Expect COBIT to see a continued evolution and broadening influence beyond IT in the next decade.

ISO

I often see confusion and misunderstanding surrounding this widely recognized acronym. ISO has the distinction of being familiar to many IT professionals, but many of these same people are not clear on what exactly ISO is today and what it is not. To start, ISO is the International Organization for Standardization. This body of authority is recognized globally for developing and publishing a broad and diverse set of international standards that apply to many industries and business types. ISO is based in Geneva, Switzerland, and works in cooperation and collaboration with many national standards-setting organizations. One example is ANSI, the American National Standards Institute. This collaborative effort results in the development of international standards that are widely published and utilized in some form by most global enterprises.

There are many ISO standards, but we will look at two examples that are most closely related to the evolution of technology, IT operations today, as well as IT governance: ISO 9000/9001 and ISO 38500.

ISO 9000/9001

For many US companies, the first experience with an ISO standard traces back to the 1980s and the introduction of a new quality management process designated ISO 9000. In the 1970s and 1980s US companies found themselves under growing pressure from non-US manufacturing firms producing relatively inexpensive products under increasingly high manufacturing standards.

US firms took notice and began to make significant changes in their manufacturing processes to achieve higher and more consistent levels of quality, and as a result be more competitive in the global marketplace.

Perhaps the best example of this shift in global quality standards is the transformation of Japanese electronics and automobiles. These products have at one time been synonymous with poor quality. All that changed when companies like Sony and Toyota achieved a dramatic transformation with regards to quality, and all global companies were forced to rethink everything.

US manufacturers began to comply with ISO 9000, which provided a single and clear standard. By nature, ISO standards are very specific and very clear. In contrast with ITIL, which provides a best practices framework that leaves room for interpretation and a somewhat versatile adoption model, ISO publishes detailed standards documents that are tightly controlled, published, and copyrighted by the ISO offices in Geneva, Switzerland. ISO is the single source of these standards.

The origins of ISO 9000 can be traced all the way back to World War II when the countries involved in the conflict were forced to achieve extraordinarily high levels of production while maintaining high levels of consistency and quality.

> *Given this production involved weapons,*
> *vehicles, ammunition, and aircraft, poor*
> *quality was not an option.*

As a result of this period and the demands placed on the manufacturing operations of the world's most prominent countries, both manufacturing processes and the associated standards changed forever.

Figure 3.16 Quality Management System

From this period emerged new models for manufacturing and also for business. One such system is the Quality Management System shown in Figure 3.16. One interesting point to note is that the rebuilding and growth of Japanese manufacturing in the 1950s and 1960s was not simply a domestic Japanese effort but involved a number of global experts, including the American W. Edwards Deming, who is widely recognized for his work in quality management. While his work would ultimately be recognized and adopted globally, Japanese firms were quick to embrace and incorporate what was then a number of completely new and revolutionary practices and standards that would change the manufacture of goods and quality forever.

By the decades of the '70s and '80s, Japanese firms had achieved significant market share of core goods, including the previous examples of automobiles and electronics, and US firms came under tremendous pressure to respond. Only then was the work of Deming and others more widely accepted.

The evolution of ISO 9000 as a collection of standards for managing quality would continue and would include:

1. Keeping detailed business records.
2. Implementing continuous improvement processes.
3. Regular reviews of processes and quality systems to measure effectiveness.
4. Monitoring production for defects and implementing corrective actions where needed.

Note the process orientation for most of this approach versus specific actions that must be taken.

Today, an enterprise may pursue ISO 9000/9001 certification as a testament to its commitment to quality. It is important to understand exactly what this certification is and what it is not. The ISO 9000 certification does not guarantee the quality of goods and products, but rather the certification addresses the application of standards in the performance of production and business processes.

The certification is of the process, not of the products or results of the process.

There are, of course, many sound reasons behind this model, but nonetheless, it remains a much discussed and debated point.

ISO 9000/9001 certification represents a significant investment on the part of an enterprise with far-reaching implications to processes and documentation. This certification can take years to complete and can only be achieved through working with a registered ISO auditor who has passed a rigorous certification of their own for a specific ISO standard set.

Today, the importance of quality and the implementation of a quality management system is understood as necessary to compete in the global marketplace. With few exceptions, every leading manufacturing company today must have achieved or be actively working toward ISO compliance.

ISO 38500

The ISO 38500 standard addresses the effective use of IT in an enterprise today and provides a framework with three objectives:

1. Providing confidence to all enterprise stakeholders in their organization's governance of IT
2. Providing guidance to managers to help govern the use of IT in their organization
3. Providing an approach for the fair and objective evaluation of the corporate governance of IT

ISO 38500 provides widespread guidance that can benefit all professionals involved in the activities of designing, implementing, and managing a corporate IT function. The standard is intended to address the needs of management and those who work closely with every level of management, including senior executives.

Relative to other ISO standards, ISO 38500 is a newcomer, with its final approval being achieved in 2008. And, unlike some other standards, ISO 38500 takes a different look at IT in very much a top-down approach that looks at how an enterprise can leverage IT versus how IT should be operated. ISO 38500 is also somewhat unique in that it looks at the responsibilities of owners, board members, and senior executives and provides a structure of governance to help fulfill legal, ethical, and regulatory obligations regarding enterprise use of IT. The standard is applicable to all organizations and lays out six principles for good corporate governance of IT:

Principle #1: Responsibility. All individuals and groups across the organization must understand and accept their responsibilities with respect to the supply of and demand for IT services and resources.

Principle #2: Strategy. A key element in an enterprise business strategy should be the current and future capabilities of IT. The execution of IT strategy must also meet the projected needs of the business strategy, each making the other strategy stronger.

Principle #3: Acquisition. All IT asset and resource acquisitions should be validated with a thorough evaluation and transparent decision-making process. Much like the financial planning process in IT Service Management, a full review of costs, benefits, and risks should be conducted with an eye to a reasonable timeline for each.

Principle #4: Performance. The performance of IT should be shaped to the needs of the enterprise and the services and service quality necessary to meet key business requirements.

Principle #5: Conformance. IT should be proactive in complying with all mandatory regulations and legislation, and to assist with audit and governance activities by maintaining records, database content, and documentation of all practices and processes.

Principle 6. Human Behavior. All IT decisions and policies should show appropriate respect for all people in the organization, including the linkages between people and the evolving needs of the business.

These principles must not be simply known, but truly embraced for ISO 38500 to be successful. To complement the six principles, ISO 38500 includes an IT Governance model shown in Figure 3.17.

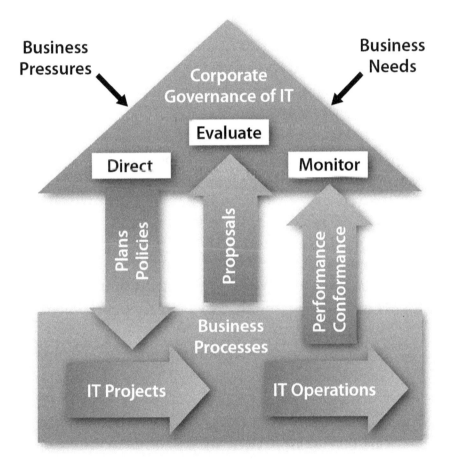

Figure 3.17 IT Governance

Like all ISO standards, ISO 38500 is not a casual endeavor and requires the full commitment of the organization, starting with senior leadership. In terms of organizational readiness for ISO,

it makes sense to create a corporate strategy for ISO, along with an ISO roadmap that takes a long-term view, five to ten years, of the ISO certifications the business will invest in and acquire successfully.

This plan sets the right expectations across the enterprise, allows the proper budgeting for the necessary investments, enables an integrated training plan, and permits the lead time needed to find ISO 38500 certified auditors and other ISO auditors who are a good fit for the business. This is an important consideration as we are looking for every possible way to improve the probability of success.

A few things to remember when implementing ISO 38500:

1. The nature of ISO 38500 demands that it be a Board level and executive priority. This is fundamental to IT governance, and the lack of this support will likely result in failure.
2. Define measurable benefits from the beginning. Compliance in the absence of these hard benefits will lose its way.
3. Identify persons in the organization as owning the certification initiative. This will likely require a team to include key business experts and an executive sponsor. The team should be incentivized to help ensure success, and one of the compliance team members should own communications. It is important the whole organization is aware of ISO certification activities and how IT will improve the business.

I have made a sincere attempt to be clear in the preceding pages that

> ***pursuit of any ISO certification is a demanding undertaking that must be backed by a significant organizational commitment and investment.***

I close this chapter with a reminder that ISO offers equally compelling value to the business and to customers served with products and services under the influence born of ISO. ISO compliance is frequently associated with market-leading enterprises that embrace the discipline and rigor demanded by ISO and recognize the many large and small improvements that will inevitably follow.

INCIDENTS

WHAT IT IS

The "A" in the ABC's of the Service Desk, an **incident** is the catalyst which creates a number of actions and business processes facilitated by the Service Desk and is supported by much of IT. Best known as an interruption to or a reduction in the performance of an IT service, the process of managing incidents is focused on restoring the service to its normal state and at the agreed-to level of quality as quickly as possible with a minimum impact on the business. It is not possible to operate a healthy Service Desk if we don't first establish a reliable Incident Management process.

WHY IT'S IMPORTANT

Incidents are a necessary part of virtually every Service

Management process and one of our Core 6 elements from Chapter 1. A few key facts to consider for Incident Management:

1. The creation of an incident is a trigger for IT Service Management.
2. Rapid resolution of incidents is critical to the business—this need is not limited to IT.
3. Critical incidents can, at their worst, shut down the business and impact revenue and customers.
4. Beyond IT Service Management, incidents can be critical to audits and governance, creating a corporate dependency on this core process.
5. Great Service Desks are great at managing incidents. This is "Ground Zero" for world-class performance.
6. A focus on incidents can be seen as old-school, but their understanding and effective management are more vital than ever.

HOW IT WORKS

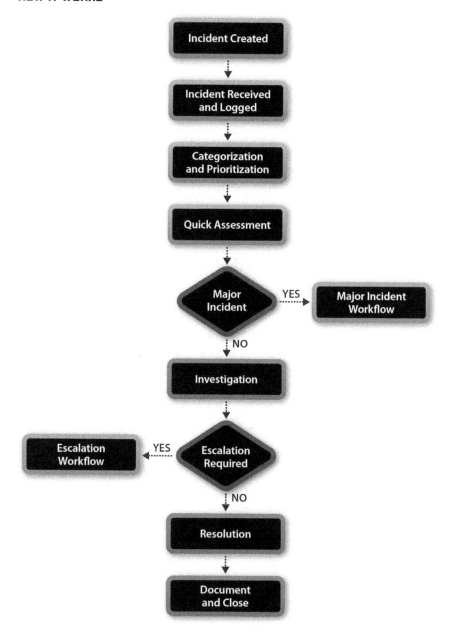

Figure 4.1 The Incident Management Process

Increasingly, the identification and creation of an incident is multi-channel. Incidents can be born by way of:

1. Phone
2. Email
3. Walk-ups
4. Self-Service
5. Service Catalog
6. Event monitoring systems

While the phone has been the most common means to create an incident for the past twenty-five years, that is now changing.

This change is being driven by two primary factors:

A. **Technology** has evolved and we now have better tools available to assist with the incident process.
B. **New expectations**, born of a new generation of worker and the dawn of the consumerization of IT, create a standard for speed and access that the phone simply can't meet.

Before we take a closer look at the incident process itself, these two important change factors need some attention, as they are driving a shift in how incidents are managed.

New technology examples that empower the incident process are email and Self-Service. While email is certainly not new, the development of tools that complement email have made a big difference, and for many organizations email is now one of the top sources of incidents. A typical scheme for an email-driven incident creation looks something like this:

1 User Sends Email to Service Desk

2 Email Listener Receives Email Real-Time

3 Email is Parsed of Key Words

4 Incident Automatically Created

5 Workflow Pushes New Incident Into Incident Process

6 Incident Management Begins

7 Standard Incident Management Process (Fig I)

8 Incident Closed

Figure 4.2 Email Incident Creation

The email listener is an application that is able to immediately (as in every minute of every day) recognize the email, utilize a parsing tool to identify keywords and content in the subject line or body of the email which can then populate an incident template, and simultaneously create and log the incident, which then triggers the standard Incident Management process. This process is convenient, as we can assume that every user in the organization has access to email, is always available in a true 24X7 model, and is very fast, as this all happens in a matter of seconds.

The Self-Service model is similar, but is more bidirectional. Self-Service is typically a portal experience that has grown rapidly in popularity because it is available 24X7, easy to use, fast, and very cost effective. The target of the Self-Service experience is the employee, or a specific customer type. For example, in education Self-Service can be an effective tool for students, and beyond the ability to open an incident, the Self-Service portal can provide access to important information, answer common questions, and manage service requests. A typical Self-Service experience looks like this:

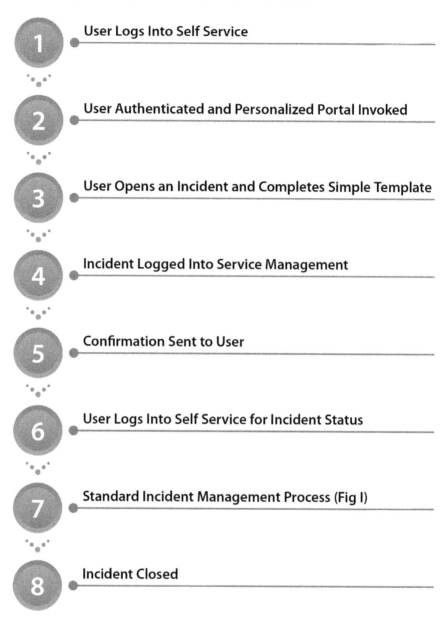

1 User Logs Into Self Service

2 User Authenticated and Personalized Portal Invoked

3 User Opens an Incident and Completes Simple Template

4 Incident Logged Into Service Management

5 Confirmation Sent to User

6 User Logs Into Self Service for Incident Status

7 Standard Incident Management Process (Fig I)

8 Incident Closed

Figure 4.3 Example Self-Service Scenario

Email and Self-Service provide options for initiating the Incident Management process, but once the incident is created, both use the standard incident workflow. This makes sense and is also necessary, as the standard structure and rigor of Incident Management are important.

Incident Creation

The creation of an incident requires some basic information that makes the incident actionable. This information can vary from organization to organization but would normally include:

1. Incident ID
2. Person logging the Incident
3. Brief description of issue
4. Incident priority
5. Related CIs
6. User contact information
7. User location
8. Time/date created

All information on the incident might not be known when it is logged, so the Incident template can be updated later in the process as more information becomes available. The initial definition provides enough of the basic elements to allow the process of Incident Management to begin. Some fields can be pre-populated when user identity is known, and this saves time and entry errors.

It is important that the incident creation process is easy for the user and as fast as possible.

One good example of a simple but impactful improvement is using pull-downs versus user-keyed fields.

Incident Received and Logged

The creation of the incident launches the Service Desk into action. Most Service Desks today utilize a Service Desk and an IT Service Management application that provides a process template for managing the incident lifecycle. Upon creation, the incident is confirmed and logged into both the process and software tool if one is in use. At this stage, incident information is verified if necessary. This is important, as the correct information on the Incident dictates both **how** and **when** actions are taken throughout the incident lifecycle.

Categorization and Prioritization

Following the logging of the incident, the category and priority of the Incident must be verified and validated. These two fields are critical to the actions throughout service management and in the standards applied to the Incident. For example, a typical priority scheme would look something like this:

P1: **Major, System Down**
P2: **Critical, Business Impacted**
P3: **Medium**
P4: **Minor**

The framework of priorities then establishes metrics, including response and resolution times that govern the timeline for actions. Expectations of organizations are growing and time is of the essence, so expect these standards to become more aggressive in the future. A typical model is as follows:

Priority	Response	Resolution
1	30 minutes	2 hours
2	1 hour	1 business day
3	2 business days	5 business days
4	5 business days	N/A

This model will vary from organization to organization depending on size, nature of business, and Service Desk resources, but what we are likely to see is some further accommodation of the P1 issues by extending the hours of response and resolution to be 24X5 or 24X7 (HoursXDays) given the nature of these incidents and the impact of a down system to the business. In some cases, these extended hours will also apply to the P2 issues and can be driven by the number of users affected. The P3 and P4 issues are likely to be managed within normal business hours.

The categorization of the incident will further drive how the incident is managed and would include at a minimum the service that is impacted and, if appropriate, the specific asset. An example categorization structure would be:

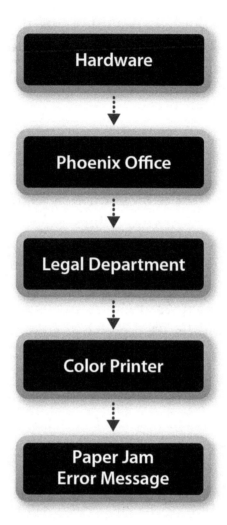

Figure 4.4 Example Incident Categorization

This categorization determines the resource assigned to the incident and can determine the escalation protocol if that becomes required. As organizations evaluate metrics and analytics, the categorization of incidents can provide insights.

Quick Assessment

The fundamental goal of Incident Management is to restore normal service as quickly as possible with minimum impact to the business. With that spirit in mind, after the incident has been logged, categorized, and prioritized, the Service Desk performs an initial assessment in an attempt to resolve the issue quickly. This is a highly desirable result and makes everybody happy. The Service Desk is motivated to achieve this first contact resolution and provide a valuable service to the business. More tools are available than ever to help the Service Management team achieve the desired result, including:

1. Knowledge Base
2. Remote Control
3. Known Errors Log

A good knowledge base provides a lot of value. Fast and effective search tools can quickly evaluate hundreds or thousands of sources and return helpful information, possible solutions, and potential workarounds. This tool can lead directly to a resolution. Another valuable tool used by the Service Desk is remote control. This tool allows the analyst to take control of the user's desktop or laptop machine and then directly observe the symptoms of the issue, evaluate further the possible causes, and implement and test potential solutions.

Remote control allows the analyst to experience the issue just as the user does and to directly observe and evaluate the environment and configuration. This is a very powerful thing, and many incidents have been closed by the first-level support team with remote control.

The known error log or database is a helpful reference for the Service Desk team. A known error is a problem that has a documented cause and a workaround has been confirmed and is in place. We will explore the "problem" part of this in more detail in the chapter on Problem Management, one of our Core 6 processes. For this discussion on the quick assessment of an Incident, the important piece is the workaround. This is a method for reducing the impact of an incident until a permanent solution is known.

> *Although a workaround is normally considered temporary, the end result to the user can be equal to that of a permanent solution.*

Remember, the goal of Incident Management is to restore normal service as quickly as possible, and with this continuously in mind, the workaround is often the best way forward. A practical way to frame this is to understand that a workaround can provide a 90 percent solution on the first call, versus waiting for the 100 percent solution to be available at some point in the future. Well, this is an easy decision for the user who is in need of help. If a permanent solution is known, that is great—it can be applied immediately and the incident is closed.

The complete incident lifecycle is currently being optimized for two factors:

1. Speed
2. User Satisfaction

Of course, speed is always a good thing assuming a successful result. A fast success is better than a slow success! This might seem obvious but we don't always focus on this measurement. Speed is a key element of world-class IT Service Management, and that is quite visible in Incident Management. Less so in other processes.

While there will always be a place for efficiency and productivity measurements for the Service Desk, expect to see a much greater focus on velocity and user satisfaction in the coming decade.

> *Speed is strategic; speed can fundamentally change our business; and speed creates competitive advantage.*

Trust me on this, my friends.

Now, to keep speed in the proper perspective, it must be balanced with a happy user. Raw speed leaving a wake of unhappy users does us little good. The pursuit of world-class Service Management can't be successful without happy users who are thrilled with the service being delivered. One way to quantify this pair of world-class metrics is 90 and 90. That would be a 90 percent reduction in the current cycle time or resolution time of an incident, along with a

90 percent user approval score. Does this seem aggressive? Certainly. Can it be done? Absolutely, and it will be met and exceeded by those organizations we will call world-class.

Investigation

If the quick assessment does not provide a fix or a work-around, the assessment transitions into a full investigation. This investigation remains focused on restoring the service as quickly as possible and utilizes the same set of tools. For example, remote control can be very effective, but there might not have been enough time, or the user might not have been available to complete the remote control session during the quick assessment. Each step of the investigation should be documented on the incident record. This is an important discipline in that it can be a critical reference as the investigation continues. And when an incident is escalated to second-level support, this team will immediately look at the incident record to review what work has been done to date. Any notes on the quick assessment can avoid wasting time and duplication of effort, and keep the process moving. This is to the benefit of both **speed** and **user satisfaction.**

Escalation

If the incident could not be resolved in the quick assessment and no solution is identified early in the investigation, the decision can be made to escalate. This is a business decision that will consider the priority and impact to the organization. In the case of an escalation, the incident moves to second-level support, where experienced and highly skilled analysts are ready to help. Normally at this time a communication protocol is followed to make the organization and management aware of the escalation. If necessary, additional resources can be applied to assist in identifying a solution. In many cases, the combination of the experienced team on second-level support and the assignment of additional resources to the escalation will result in a rapid resolution.

> *World-class organizations are very focused on the governing SLA, speed of action, and restoring normal service to the user.*

When rallying around an escalation, there are a number of things that will happen. Note our use of the word *rally* here. The behavior we should expect is a strong, focused, and high-energy response to the escalation that has widespread visibility across the organization. The incident is by definition of relative importance, and world-class organizations will nurture a mind-set of doing "whatever it takes" to get the escalated issue resolved.

Beyond the attention of the second-level support team, there are a few additional actions that can enhance the escalation process, including:

1. Executive sponsorship
2. Incentives
3. Assignment of Development/R&D/Engineering resources

Executive sponsorship of critical escalated incidents is recommended and has a few clear benefits. First, the executive sponsor can raise the visibility of the issue with the management team and help accelerate the timeline of response. Yes, that *speed* thing again! The executive sponsor also demonstrates the commitment of the organization to the rapid resolution of the issue. Good communication is an important element of the escalation process (and of Incident Management as a whole), and the executive sponsor can assist with the communication internally across the cross-functional teams, and with any updates to the user or customer.

Yet another benefit of this sponsorship model is that executives are often in the best position to negotiate "internally" to apply additional resources to the escalation. This can include money and people. More on that in the coming paragraphs.

We all have an innate desire to be recognized and praised.

Tapping into this desire can be an effective tool for the business while creating a compelling opportunity for the team working on the escalation. Incentives can be as simple as verbal or email recognition with the team or a broader audience in the company. Yes, this is simple, but also very important and effective. Another option is a not-too-expensive but fun gift, like action cameras, activity trackers, high-quality headphones, wireless speakers, and multi-tools. Remember, we are trying to generate another level of excitement and energy to be applied to the escalation, and gifts of this type can make that happen. And of course there is the option of a cash bonus. Cash is timeless, something everybody appreciates and responds well to. The gift or the cash bonus should be presented publicly when possible to allow the individual to enjoy the well-deserved recognition.

In most organizations, domain experts, technology experts, and specialized skills exist outside the Support organization. These valuable skills can be working day-to-day in development, engineering, operations, security, research, governance, or consulting organizations.

> *The timely assignment of the right resource can accelerate the resolution of an escalated incident.*

And in most cases these people enjoy the opportunity to help the business and to step outside their normal role for a while. The key is in recognizing the need for a skillset that matches the nature of the incident, identifying the right person(s) in the organization, contacting the right manager to make the person(s) available to work the escalation, and ensuring adequate time is allocated to come up to speed on the incident. A fresh-look investigation is valuable and can ultimately result in the identification and implementation of a solution.

History has shown that when these highly skilled and knowledgeable people are deployed on an escalation, the probability of success is very high. Because the rate of success is high, *it is important that discretion is used in deploying these valuable people at the right time, no more often and no less often than absolutely necessary*

to have an impact on the most urgent or strategic escalations. This is world-class behavior. Note that it is important to recognize both the manager who agreed to release the expert to work on the escalation and the person who identified the ultimate solution. This sets the right tone for a strong escalation process, drives the right behavior across the organization, enforces the right priorities, and sets a precedent for the next time such a need arises and we are ready to rally around the cause.

Resolution

Whether it be through the standard Incident Management process with the first-level support team, or through the escalation process at second-level, third-level support, or an extended team of experts, a possible solution will be identified and the incident process then works through steps to validate the resolution. These steps will include:

1. Preliminary testing performed to verify the solution
2. Additional use cases applied to broaden testing
3. Users contacted to participate in testing or to validate the solution
4. Solution implemented

Quick-look testing is done during the identification of a possible fix and as an immediate step toward verifying the solution. If the fix looks promising, it is best to acquire use cases from the originating user and if possible to involve the user in the testing process. This is good for everybody. It creates a reality-based test process, because nobody knows the incident better and is in a better position to verify "normal service" than the user. User involvement will also increase the confidence of the escalation or first-level support team that a solution has in fact been identified. And in the interest of speed, speed, speed, it is also highly likely the involvement will save precious time.

With the fix verified, it is then implemented and put into daily use. For the purposes of this discussion on Incident Management, we have simplified this step, but in practice it should be noted this step of implementation may be subject to the Change Management and Release Management processes.

Document and Close

It is not easy, and it is not convenient, but it is absolutely necessary to bring the incident record up to date and to document the steps, findings, what worked and did not work, timing of actions, and any other pertinent information that should be included. This is also an opportunity to identify content that should be added to the knowledge base as a knowledge article that can then support the resolution of future incidents. With this mind-set, and recognizing this opportunity to feed the right information into the knowledge base, we will see ongoing improvement of this valuable asset.

This documentation can be used in many ways, including in training, trend analysis, future root cause analysis, and management reporting.

It is not unusual to be moving quickly to find a solution and the information on the incident record/file falls behind the current state of things. This is okay, but only temporarily. World-class organizations will have a standard window within which the incident should be updated to the documentation standard and then closed following the resolution of the issue. Something like five business days is about right. This is an important organizational discipline and must be recognized and enforced by management.

KEY INTEGRATIONS AND PARTNERSHIPS FOR INCIDENTS

1. Problem Management: establish and maintain the relationship between incidents and problems, including the information and systems that can provide this information on a regular basis.
2. Availability Management: assessment of all incidents that impact service availability and planning with availability managers to determine how to best prevent similar problems in the future.
3. Change Management: work with Change Managers to understand and maintain visibility of changes that will address incidents and problems.
4. Knowledge Management: coordinate with Knowledge Managers to develop and execute the plan to provide knowledge base access at the time an incident is created and throughout the incident

lifecycle. It is also important that we are proactive with Knowledge Management in delivering the right information from the front lines of Incident Management into the knowledge base so it continues to be enriched over time.

TIPS FOR SUCCESSFUL INCIDENT MANAGEMENT

1. Commit to being great at managing incidents. Greatness is built from the ground up, and remember, world-class IT Service Management starts here.
2. Focus on speed. Resolving the incident is no longer enough; it must be done quickly.
3. Leverage Self-Service technologies to offload the Service Desk and to save time and money.
4. Create a method to accurately measure user satisfaction. This and speed are above all else.
5. Invest in a well-understood and optimized Major/P1 Incident workflow. The Service Desk must be at its very best for these issues that pose a real threat to the business.
6. Be judicious with escalations and when necessary mobilize swiftly and strongly. Leverage executive sponsorship, incentives, and domain experts to get results quickly.

CHAPTER 5

SERVICE REQUESTS

Service requests broaden the scope and role of the traditional ticket or today's incident. This recognizes the evolution of IT Service Management and the processes and needs of users moving far beyond the Break-Fix model. Expect the role of service requests to grow and diversify in the years ahead as driven by the evolving needs of users and customers in combination with the ascension of IT in the business. To explore this further than what I provide in this chapter, see the chapters on Service Catalog (Chapter 6) and Enterprise Service Management (Chapter 17).

WHAT IT IS

The service request captures a user question, need for information, standard change, or the use of a new service. This request then becomes a catalyst for a series of actions designed to fulfill the request in a manner that is a good use of resources while meeting or exceeding the fundamental needs of the requester. Both the request and the fulfillment process should be flexible, recognizing the highly dynamic and diversified nature of the service request.

WHY IT IS IMPORTANT

A service request allows the Service Desk to deliver a broad range of services and to quickly capture the changing needs of the organization. Some models will mix incidents with service requests, but I don't recommend this. An incident is an incident and a service request is a service request; they are not the same and are supported by a very different set of actions and requirements. Let's keep this simple. Service requests offer a number of benefits to the organization:

1. To increase the speed and convenience of user access to services
2. To increase user satisfaction by answering questions and providing access to commonly requested information
3. To improve the productivity and effectiveness of the complete organization by providing the right information and the right service at the right time
4. Better control of service fulfillment by working through a standard and consistent channel for each request
5. Reduced costs associated with delivering common services by providing pre-defined processes and quick approvals ready to fulfill the request
6. To grow the visibility of services by providing common and simple interfaces for all users to make a request at any time

HOW IT WORKS

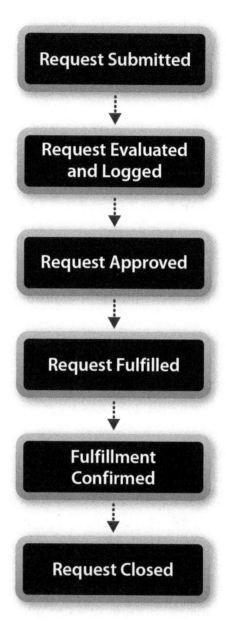

Figure 5.1 The Service Request Process

Request Submitted

The first step with a service request is an important one. We want our customers and users to have a good experience, to get what they need, and to get it quickly. This will, of course, allow our users to be at their best and to come back to IT the next time a service can enable them to do their job better. Flexibility is part of the good start equation.

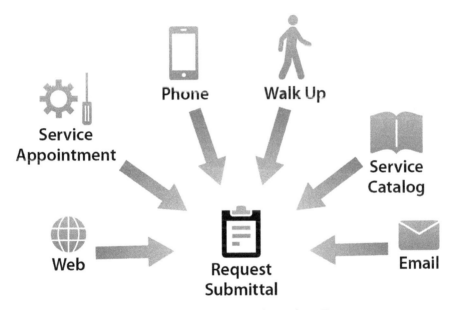

Figure 5.2 Submitting a Service Request

It should be easy to submit the request while at the same time accommodating different user styles and different user needs. From the service request has sprung a more diverse set of channels through which we can make the request. This evolution has been influenced extensively by the Consumerization of IT (Chapter 18) and the ability to automate the request and fulfillment processes (Chapter 16). This is an exciting development, as it has resulted in the beginning of the realization of our vision for Fast and Easy, two of our key principles for world-class IT Service Management.

Back to the methods shown in Figure 5.1, the phone is our original method and needs no explanation.

> *The Service Catalog was built expressly for the purpose of fulfilling service requests and is a rising star in IT Service Management today.*

This topic is important enough to be discussed in detail in Chapter 6 and earned a place as one of our Core 6 elements.

It is worth noting here that after thirty years of the phone standing as the number-one form of contact with the Service Desk, it will soon, if not already, be displaced by Web Methods (Gartner Group, March 2015) and this trend is likely to accelerate with the fastest growing channels being Web portals and Service Catalog. If we add email to the mix, Web contacts have exceeded the phone today.

At the same time, service requests have become the fastest growing segment of issues coming to the Service Desk, and while the traditional Break/Fix remains necessary, it is a slower channel and users are seeking alternatives for a needed service. This is not to imply that Break/Fix is no longer critical but rather a reflection of the growing diversity of services offered by the Service Desk and this team no longer being limited to fixing problems in a tactical manner.

***The combination of these facts further sup-
ports the fundamental transformation of
the Service Desk.***

Request Evaluated and Logged

The service request form should be as simple as possible. Remember, many service request submitters are non-technical users, and we want to make the process a good experience. And there are other benefits to a simple service request form.

A simple request form is fast, it is easy, and it is less error prone. This reduces wasted time and rework in the request fulfillment process. This in turn reduces the overall costs of offering a service. It also makes the evaluation of a request by IT much faster. We are checking to be sure all required fields are completed, and where possible the form should include pull-down menus and auto-fill fields, which saves more time and further reduces input errors.

With all fields completed, the request is logged into the service request business process, which in turn triggers the next steps. A Request Priority has been assigned and confirmed, and this value is used during the workflow process to prioritize the request against other requests and to make decisions around resource assignments and the timeline of fulfillment. This priority ensures we are meeting the expectations of our customers/users while at the same time making good and smart use of assets and resources. Throughout the fulfillment process we should leverage automation tools to optimize both the time required and manual participation in the request process.

Even small time savings provided by automation add up to significant time and cost savings over time.

Request Approved

Many service requests will be preapproved. But given that every request has a cost associated with it, the cost must be understood and an approval will be required for requests that are not preapproved. This is a good thing for several reasons:

1. Approvals for higher cost requests support cost accountability.
2. Approvals and tracking allow us to assign costs to specific organizations and understand the cost of operations.
3. There is an increased visibility of the users consuming services and the relative demand for each service.

Approvals are necessary, but this creates the risk of wasted time. The approval process should be automated to the greatest extent possible. For example, if the cost of a service request is over the preapproval limit, we can use a workflow model to send an automated email immediately to a primary approver. This is very cool, but it gets even better. At the instant the email is sent, we can start an automatic timer that tracks the elapsed time waiting for the approval.

Then, if a predefined limit is exceeded, we can send a second email to an alternate approver. And, of course, this model could be extended further if needed.

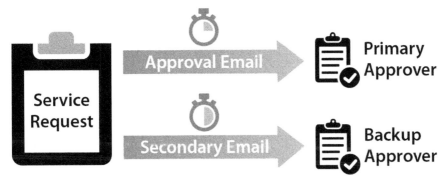

Figure 5.3 Automated Service Request Approval

At first glance this might not seem like a big deal, but it really makes a difference over time, saving hours and potentially days for each request requiring an approval. Let's look at this a little closer—there are at least six work segments in this sequence that can potentially save us time:

1. Initial email sent instantly
2. Waiting for initial approval
3. Upon approval, service request is released into the fulfillment process
4. Secondary email sent instantly when primary timer is exceeded
5. Waiting for secondary approval
6. Upon approval, service request is released into the fulfillment process

With the potential of wasted minutes or hours in each of these steps, the workflow model can ensure we don't lose a second. A prudent estimate is that this automation will save us an average of two hours per approval process. If we then assume only 100 service requests per month (some organizations are now doing thousands of requests per month), this saves us 200 valuable hours per month. This is twenty-five business days of recovered time!

Request Fulfilled

This process is the complete delivery of the service requested. It can be as simple as answering a question or taking feedback on a user experience with an existing service. Or it can be a more complex process that requires an approval.

An example of the second type of process would be installation of a software application on a user laptop. This is also a good candidate for automation. Let's look at the steps of this fulfillment.

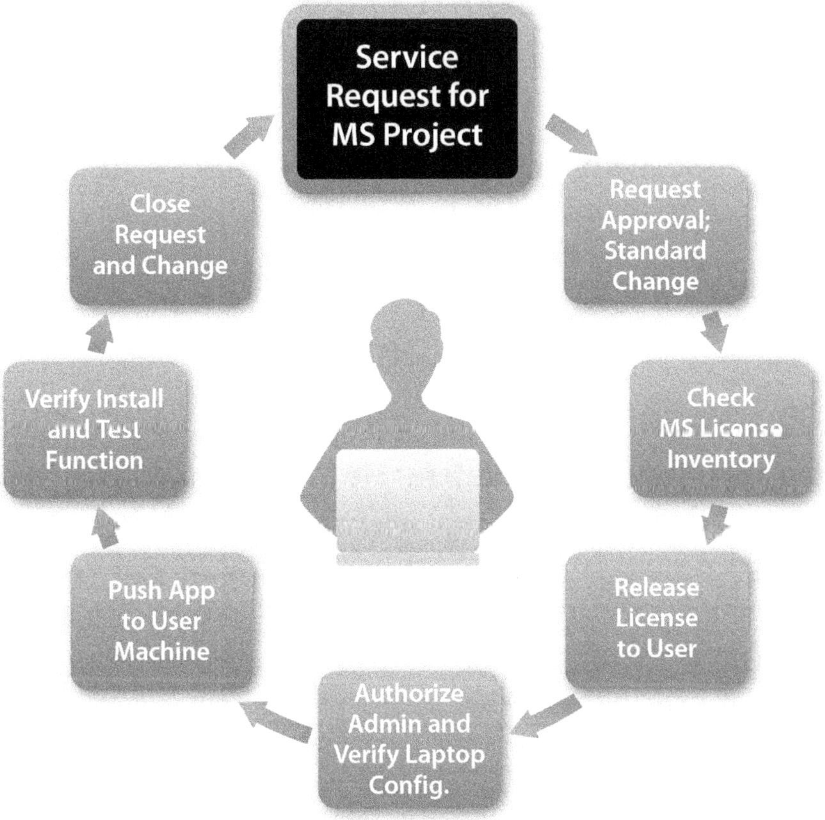

Figure 5.4 Service Request for Application Install

With the right Service Management and Client Management software tools, most of this process can be automated and completed in a matter of minutes. In the past, this process could require a full business day or more. This is very much in line with the key world-class IT Service Management principle of speed. I make this point repeatedly throughout the book because it is both critical to world-class performance and not a traditional priority in IT Service Management.

The birth and growth of the Help Desk in the 1980s and

1990s came with a focus on efficiency, labor costs, and staff productivity. While these metrics have a place today,

> *Our emphasis in IT Service Management has evolved, and factors including speed, personalized service, Me-Level support, and ease of access to services will shape the future.*

These themes will then shape both how we offer services and how we fulfill a service request. How we fulfill will continue to change and technology will move forward, but we will always be grounded by a focus on the speedy delivery of a quality service—resulting in a thrilled user or customer. It just does not get any better than that, and this is at the heart of a strong Service Desk.

Fulfillment Confirmed

It is important that we make it easy and convenient to submit a service request, to get it approved if necessary, and then to execute the fulfillment of the request. We don't have a good process if both the front-end and the fulfillment are not strong.

However, this is not enough.

> *We have an equally important responsibility at the back-end of the process*

in following up with the user to ensure they have

everything they need and the service provided, however large or small, met or exceeded expectations. It's not easy to take the time to complete the follow-up, as there are new service requests that need attention, but this must be done, and it is an organizational discipline that we must commit to. What I see work best is a two-touch follow-up. The first touch should be immediately after the delivery of the service is completed. This is to make sure everything is okay and to address any final issues or questions. This allows us to catch anything that is not quite right and make it right before frustration has a chance to grow and we have an unhappy user.

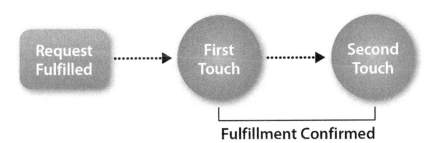

Fulfillment Confirmed

Figure 5.5 Service Request Two-Touch Follow-up

The second touch should be two to four weeks later to confirm there are no new issues or questions related to the service request that need to be addressed. The user will appreciate the follow-up; this communication will aid the Service Desk in preventing any potential confusion and in catching any spin-offs of the original request early and while they are likely easy to address. This two-touch process will also improve communication that is a source of user dissatisfaction. The touch points take only a few minutes and can significantly enhance customer satisfaction and create an increasingly proactive service model. What's not to like?

Request Closed

Most Service Desks will close the request after the first confirmation and then do the second touch point as a scheduled task and update the original service request record if needed. However, it is perfectly acceptable to close the request only after the second confirmation is completed. This is simply a matter of which model fits your organization and process best.

> *What is more important is ensuring the service request record is updated with any and all feedback received from the user.*

This is a valuable reference in the days and weeks following the completion of the service request and also well into the future to support reporting, metrics, and the analysis of performance for all service requests and specific categories of requests. A good example of the opportunity to learn is capturing any feedback in the knowledge base, which supports training activities but also improves our analysis and reporting of past successes and challenges.

We can learn a lot from the analysis of historical service requests, but this is only possible with complete and accurate information added to the service request record. This is another example of a necessary organizational discipline and part of the steps from good, to great, to world-class.

A note about updating the form or record associated with the objects in our Core 6 or World-Class 12 processes, whether it is an incident record, a problem record, a change request, or the service requests from this chapter:

It is vital that we set the expectation from the very beginning of our journey that this is something we must do well.

It is not optional. Most of us don't get excited about taking notes and updating documentation of any type. This is perfectly understandable, and given the choice, it is something we simply would not do. But make no mistake, the notes and comments added to our process records during the daily work done in support of the twelve processes described in this book hold the key to learning, the key to understanding history, the key to getting better, and absolutely necessary to our journey to world-class IT Service Management.

We will establish throughout this book that "world class" is not about doing one or two big things incredibly well. It is about doing a bunch of things a little better every day; to commit our culture to a journey in pursuit of excellence and to do so with passion and integrity that in turn create the energy that allows us to continue the journey. This simple point on documenting requests and user feedback on a service request does not seem like a big deal in itself, but it is yet another reminder of the core sustaining principle that we live every day.

KEY INTEGRATIONS AND PARTNERSHIPS FOR SERVICE REQUESTS

1. Service Portfolios: Coordination and collaboration to determine the set of currently active service requests and how they will be offered to users and customers. Look forward to plan for the future offering of new services and the associated service requests.

2. Service Catalog: Service Request Managers will work closely with the Service Catalog Manager to verify all service requests to be offered in the catalog and the level of service and SLA associated with each.

3. Non-IT Business Owners: Develop a partnership to determine what service requests can be defined and offered to the business beyond IT. Recognize the synergies across multiple non-IT departments offering reuse of service request templates and workflows.

4. Service Level Management: For each request to be offered and received, coordinate with both the Service Portfolio Manager and the Service Catalog Manager to confirm the level of service and SLA for each request that can be received from a user or customer.

TIPS FOR SUCCESSFUL SERVICE REQUESTS

1. It must be easy to view all services available to a user or customer and to request the service we need.

2. Design the service request process with no limits. This process, in combination with Service Catalog, will become a primary channel for the future of service delivery, and we don't want to hit artificial limits later. It is much easier to plan for growth from the beginning.

3. Clearly define service requests that are preapproved and those that require an approval process.

4. Leverage automation for the approval and request fulfillment process. This will save precious time and resources. Speed is essential, and slowness kills user satisfaction.

5. Listen carefully to user/customer feedback. This is how we get better and identify new service requests for the future.

6. Service request records must be updated with current and accurate notes on the good and the bad. Accept nothing less.

CHAPTER 6

SERVICE CATALOG

Service Catalog is a fascinating process. It has seen a remarkable evolution in the past five years and is expected to have a significant influence over the reshaping of IT in the decade ahead. From the pragmatic beginnings of a simple list or catalog of services offered by IT, the Service Catalog is now so much more, including a catalyst to key initiatives in IT: Service Automation (Chapter 16), Enterprise Service Management (Chapter 17), and the Consumerization of IT (Chapter 18). This is a great example of why IT Service Management has become such an important partner to the business and a strategic enabler to our future. Something from our traditional IT Service Desk has become something new and driving remarkable change that is not limited to IT, but rather reaching across the business and all the way to our customers. With this unique profile and trajectory in mind, I have included Service Catalog in the Core 6 processes. This is a selection that I'm sure some will question because it is certainly not in line with some old-school IT perceptions of Service Catalog, but it makes a lot of sense as we explore the current state and future of world-class IT Service Management. Done well, the influences of Service Catalog across the business can be remarkable and provide us with another glimpse of purest ray serene where many least expect to find it, amongst the machinations of humble IT.

WHAT IT IS

The Service Catalog is the current and definitive source of all available services. Service Catalog is a subset of the Service Portfolio, which also contains inactive services and future services that are not yet available. The Service Catalog provides a reliable and consistent view of all services available to the users and customers approved for access and to request and consume the service.

WHY IT IS IMPORTANT

The nature of Service Catalog is such that it provides both **tactical** and **strategic** benefits to the business. This is a unique quality of this process and another reason it is included in our Core 6 processes. Following are some good examples of the benefits we receive from Service Catalog:

1. Service Catalog provides a consistent and single view of all services currently offered by IT.
2. Service Catalog, when presented correctly, can provide a friendly and convenient way to request a service across a diverse base of customers with very different needs.

3. Service Catalog is a great opportunity to partner with the business and offer both IT and non-IT services that leverage the same process and same tools.

4. Service Catalog creates an ideal opportunity to leverage automation that can result in both higher customer satisfaction and a lower cost of fulfillment. In the past, these two things were considered mutually exclusive, and we are now able to shatter that traditional perception for the first time.

5. The new generation of Service Catalog software tools can provide an attractive and fast user experience that puts a new face on IT and changes the perception of IT across the business. It is not an exaggeration to say this changes everything, and it often begins with the Service Catalog.

6. An accurate Service Catalog greatly reduces wasted time and increases customer satisfaction by ensuring all services viewed in the catalog are up to date and ready to be delivered.

7. The Service Catalog can define and bring needed attention to dependencies across the business, including those between services, with people resources, and with assets and CI's necessary to deliver a quality service quickly. These dependencies can then be managed for the necessary level of health and availability.

HOW IT WORKS

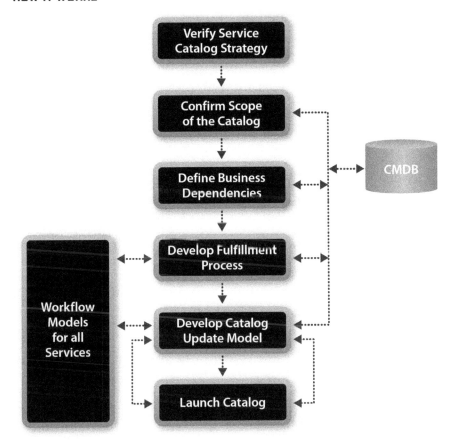

Figure 6.1 Overview of Service Catalog

Verify Service Catalog Strategy

As we prepare to offer the Service Catalog to the business and potentially to customers, a strategy for the catalog will help ensure a successful launch and successful operations following. The strategy will provide needed guidance and help to answer a few key questions:

1. Which services will be offered in the catalog and when should they be offered?
2. Will a single consolidated catalog meet the need or will we require a business Service Catalog plus a technical Service Catalog?
3. Who will the catalog be offered to and how will access be provided?
4. Is there an adequate definition of how each service will be fulfilled?
5. Will there be a charge or cost model for the services offered in the catalog?
6. Will there be any approval required for services requested through the catalog?
7. What are the key metrics to be used to evaluate Service Catalog performance and how will they be published?
8. What are the interfaces and integrations required for the catalog to operate successfully?
9. What is the scope of the organization(s) to be supported by the catalog and what is the mapping of services to each organization?

Some of these questions are easy to answer, some not so much. In either case the strategy will provide the guidance needed to make the best use of this strategic process. For example, a decision must be made from the beginning on what services from the full-service portfolio should be offered in the Service Catalog. In some cases it can make sense to offer a core set of services, those in highest demand or those with the greatest impact to the business. I see the most success when a limited number of services are offered in phase one to validate the fulfillment model and to get some experience with the front-end (assuming the company is using a software application for the user experience). And then when this model is running well, the scope can be expanded to include additional services.

The strategy does not need to be a long document but should provide the context of what the primary goals of the catalog are and how it supports the business.

Confirm Scope of the Catalog

While the Service Catalog strategy will provide guidance on the scope of the catalog at a higher level, the need remains to create a roster of each service to be included in the catalog.

> *This final list of service requests will be co-ordinated with Service Level Management, with Service Portfolio, and with the Service Request Managers. These dependencies and partnerships are important.*

Service Level Management will confirm and help define the level of service required for each item in the catalog, including SLAs. Service Portfolio Management will assist in defining the services that should and should not be in scope for the catalog, and the service request team will provide the details for both the request itself and the fulfillment/workflow back-end. With all of this in place, we can move closer to launching the catalog.

Yes, there will be another set of actions necessary at a finer level of detail, but this definition of scope helps to focus our attention and resources on the service requests to go live and the infrastructure around them to create a responsive and reliable catalog. Note that throughout this discussion where there is an assumption you are likely using a software application, in most cases an IT Service Management product will assist in the creation, launch, and daily operation of the catalog. These tools have improved dramatically in the past ten years, and the best tools will include a Service Catalog module. We will come back to this later in the chapter.

Define Business Dependencies

The successful operation of the Service Catalog requires a coordinated effort from an extended team. Any dependencies across the organization must be defined and owners assigned to ensure all the necessary elements are functioning at a high level when needed. The Service Catalog has a front-end, which is the presentation of the catalog to the customer, and a back-end, which includes the information for each service offered, and the fulfillment business process or workflow models that capture what happens between the moment a customer requests a service and the moment the service has been successfully completed. The front-end and back-end are very different in nature, but both are critical to the success of the catalog.

Launching the Service Catalog is a significant investment, and taking this on without a good plan—and owners assigned to each deliverable for the front-end and the back-end—is folly.

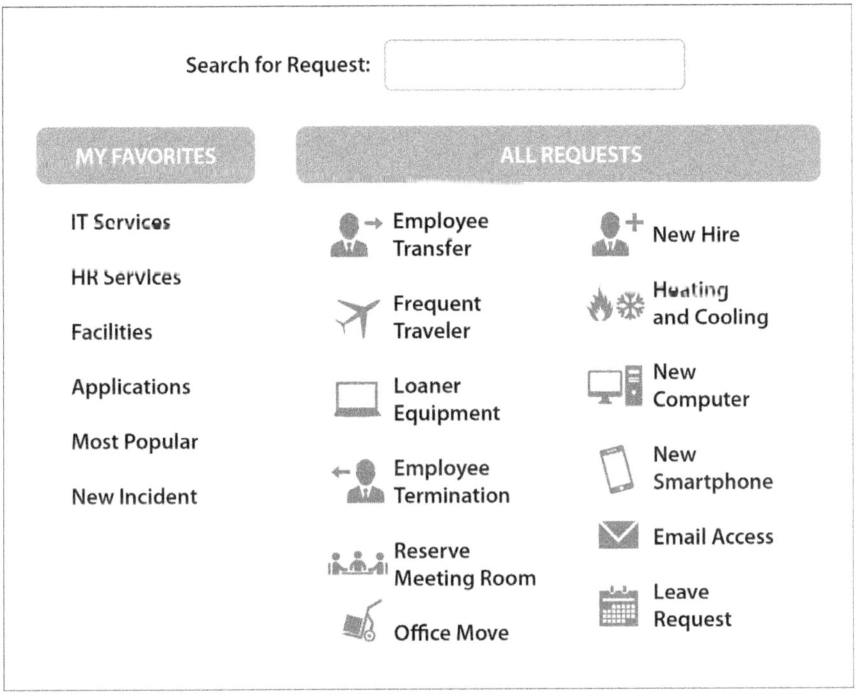

Figure 6.2 Example Service Catalog User Experience

Figure 6.2 shows an example of the user experience at the front-end of requesting a service. This is a simple illustration that provides a search feature, access to favorite services used in the past, and then a list of all services available. These services can be filtered for relevance based on the ID and organization of the current user.

The goal of this front-end is to make requesting a service

easy, convenient, and fast. We explore this theme more in Chapter 18, the Consumerization of IT Service Management, but this is all about moving beyond the traditional looks-like-IT, feels-like-IT type of experience to something that is for the business and intuitive for business users. Note the contents of the catalog in our simple example of twelve services. We see a mix of IT, HR, facilities, and travel-related requests. This is just the beginning and gives you a glimpse into why Service Catalog is driving change across the business and changing the perception of IT in the organization.

> *This is not just about a friendly user experience for Service Catalog; this is about driving velocity in the business, which creates happy customers and results in a positive impact on revenue.*

The example in Figure 6.2 also highlights the dependencies that are in place in order to fulfill the service request—these go beyond IT to include HR Managers and Facilities Managers and the Corporate Travel Office. These teams must understand:

1. Their team plays a role in delivering the service
2. The specific actions to be taken to assist in delivering the service
3. The anticipated volume of requests expected
4. What information must be provided to the non-IT team to enable them to take their actions
5. The process and communications to be used in the event there is a problem with fulfillment/delivery

6. The SLAs in place for the service in question and any reporting or metrics that are required

These points, together with the overall design of the fulfill-ment process, will enable the next step.

Define Fulfillment Process

With the dependencies defined and the overall design of the fulfillment process in place, we can define the details of the fulfillment workflow for each service to be offered in the Service Catalog. The catalog should not go live until such time as we have a rock-solid understanding of how we deliver the requested service in a way that is consis-tent, reliable, and efficient with our resources. What I see repeatedly is success designed into the fulfillment process through careful planning and communication, resulting in a very clear and detailed description of the business pro-cess to deliver every service offered in the catalog. These organizations are consistently successful. Conversely, oth-er organizations move quickly forward with no accurate definition of how a service will be delivered, due to sched-ule pressures or simply a lack of commitment to this step. These organizations are certainly not doomed to fail, but they have accepted a greater level of risk that problems will occur when requests are raised from the Service Catalog. As a general practice, every opportunity to reduce risk should be taken, and this is a good example of where we should invest the necessary time.

The fulfillment process begins with a customer select-ing a Service and completing a request form that provides necessary information to the first steps of the business process to deliver the service. Simple is best. Let's look at the example for a new hire request:

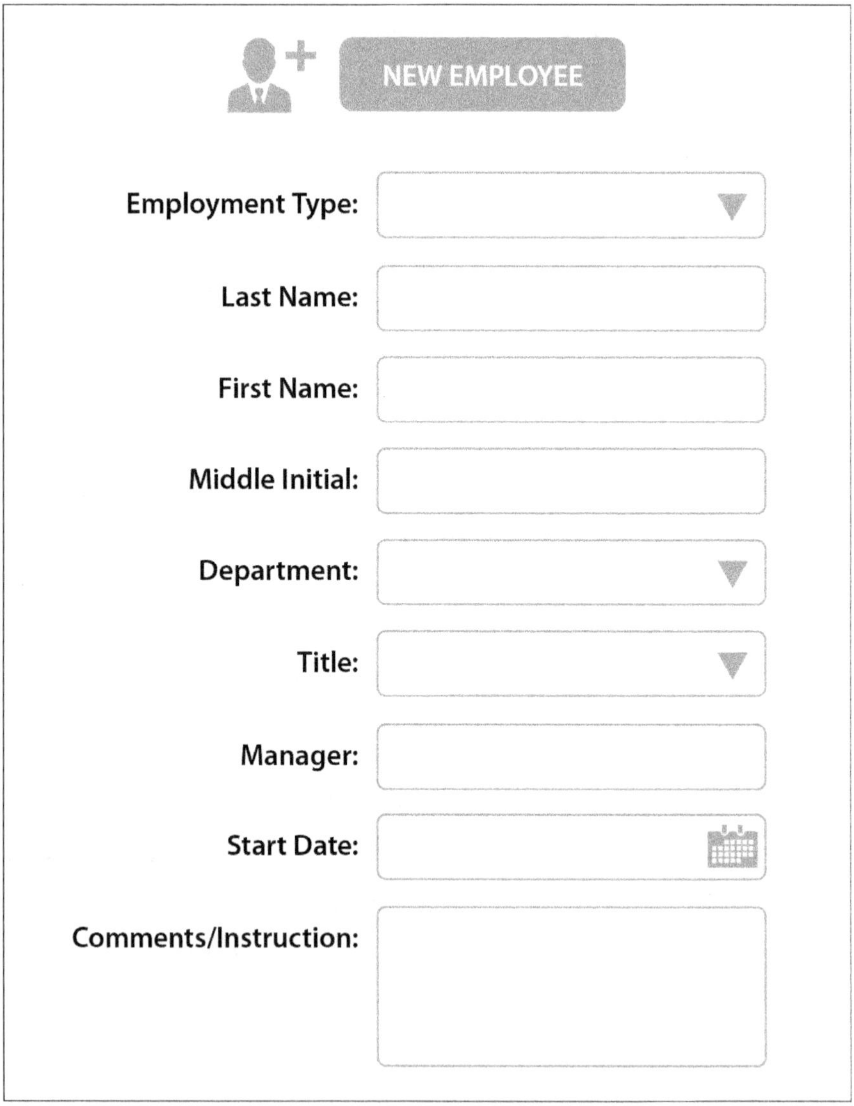

NEW EMPLOYEE

Employment Type:

Last Name:

First Name:

Middle Initial:

Department:

Title:

Manager:

Start Date:

Comments/Instruction:

Figure 6.3 Service Catalog New Hire Request

With this information completed, the workflow is triggered

to start. I provided examples of business rules and work-flow models in Chapter 16 on Service Automation. With the widespread availability of IT Service Management software applications, I have assumed throughout the book that vir-tually all Service Desks today are leveraging software tools to both offer the Service Catalog to customers and to auto-mate as much of the fulfillment process as possible.

This makes sense given how good these tools have become and the time and resource savings available. This theme ap-pears throughout not just Chapter 16 but also Chapter 17 on Enterprise Service Management, Chapter 5 on Service Requests, and Chapter 18 on the Consumerization of IT Service Management.

> *This is a good time to remember that be-fore we can leverage automation, business rules, and workflow tools, it is necessary to first understand the fulfillment process,*

to create a document that describes and sketches the pro-cess step-by-step, socialize this working definition to all the teams and individuals that have a role in the process, get the necessary feedback and make these changes to the document, and finally to get the sign-off from the extended team. Yes, this is a manual process in the beginning, using paper and whiteboards or a flowchart tool. This definition must include every step, decision points if any, inputs and outputs from every step, and backup or secondary steps where they exist.

With this model in place we can be confident of being well prepared to deliver to all requests coming through the Service Catalog. At this point some planning should be done on scalability—how can we fulfill service requests if demand doubles? If demand increases by 5X? By 10X? You get the idea. This is a healthy exercise, assuming success and growth and something that does not require a lot of time but can save a lot of time later should we need to mobilize more assets and more people to scale up the catalog.

Develop Catalog Update Model

The Service Catalog will be a living entity and will change over time. New services will be added, services will be retired, and existing services will be modified, including how they are fulfilled. The ability to make these changes will be greatly improved if we design-in the flexibility from the beginning. Trying to make this work well after the catalog has been live for a period of time is much more difficult.

> *We can take advantage of some of the pre-launch work and apply it to the catalog update model, but the creation of the catalog is different than what it will take to keep the catalog in line with the current state of the business.*

A few cases to be considered and a few questions that need to be answered:

1. What is the procedure to add a new service to the catalog, including testing and final approval(s)?
2. What is the procedure to remove an existing service from the catalog, including the final authorization(s)?
3. How are changes made to an existing request in the catalog and how are requests of the same type that are already in process managed?
4. How are updates to the Service Catalog communicated to customers?
5. What reports will be published to include which metrics and on what schedule to update IT management on the performance of the Service Catalog?
6. Following the go-live of the Service Catalog, a document that provides a template for the design of the service and the fulfillment process should be published as a reference.
7. Normally, the Service Catalog Manager will own facilitating answers to these questions and publishing the guide in #6.
8. A coordination agreement, even if it is informal, must be in place between the Service Catalog Manager and the Service Portfolio Manager regarding the addition, removal, and all changes to services in the Catalog.
9. If costs or cross-charging is in the scope of the catalog, any updates to the catalog must include a cross-check on the cost data.
10. Any updates to the catalog must include a review of the SLAs for that service and an associated update if required.

No single one of these sample items will make or break the

update process for the Service Catalog, but if each is not measured and managed as needed, the value of the catalog will erode over time. This is a reminder of the unique multi-dimensional nature of the catalog, and it comes with a large responsibility to thoughtfully manage the evolution of the catalog, which in turn sustains the exciting impact the catalog can have on the business.

Launch Catalog

With the strategy, scope, dependencies, and fulfillment processes defined and in place and the update model understood, it is time to launch the catalog. Given the broad visibility of the catalog and the investment of time and resources made to get to this point, we want to take some additional care to ensure a successful launch. A few things to incorporate into the final steps and considerations to reduce risk:

1. Run a pilot program to identify any final issues.
2. Launch with a limited set of services for phase I before scaling up to a full set of requests.
3. Validate the support model for the new catalog.
4. Be proactive in getting feedback from customers in phase I and make adjustments quickly.
5. Verify the customer experience.

No amount of preparation can completely de-risk the launch of the catalog, so I like to see a pilot program run with a select group of customers. This will drive out any initial issues and avoid a broader exposure with the full go-live. Ensure the customers have the right expectations in the pilot and understand what is expected of them. It is important to select a few customers with the right mind-set and understand the difference between the pilot and the production system. This does not need to be a long process; two to four weeks can be effective.

It is a good practice to take a phased approach to the services offered in the catalog.

About ten to fifteen core services work well for a phase I. Even in the case of a catalog that will ultimately include hundreds of service requests, I recommend starting with a modest phase I. This greatly increases the probability of success and enables IT to respond quickly to any issues and make the necessary adjustments before scaling up the number of service requests in the catalog. Select services for phase I that are well understood from a fulfillment standpoint and are high volume or high value to the business. We specify the latter because we do want to attach strong benefits to phase I, and we can certainly achieve this with a little planning, even with our modest scope. Resist the temptation to stuff more into phase I!

Before the launch we need to verify the support model for the catalog. Will issues and questions go to the same queue as all other calls? Or will any Service Catalog incidents go to a dedicated group of analysts? This decision is based on a number of factors, and there is no one right answer. What is important is the validation of the model prior to the launch to enable the support team to be prepared and deliver a great support experience to your customers. Another consideration is to recognize that the Service Catalog invokes strong reactions, and we will receive comments and enhancement requests from customers along with true incidents and how-to requests.

This is all good, and the tracking system should collect these requests to be reviewed and considered for future enhancement releases of the catalog.

> *Feedback from customers is a great source of ideas for how to improve the Service Catalog, and it is important from a relationship standpoint that the voice of the customer is heard.*

As the Service Catalog goes live, it is necessary to be proactive in seeking customer feedback. Yes, it is true that feedback will eventually make its way back to the Service Catalog Manager, but this is a recipe for customer frustration. A proactive outreach changes the customer mind-set and goes a long way to defuse frustrations and create more of a partnership discussion. This makes life better for everybody. A few points to cover with customers:

1. We see that you requested a service today out of the Service Catalog. How was your experience?
2. What did you like best about your experience?
3. How can we improve your experience in the future?
4. Was there anything you needed that you could not find?
5. We would appreciate any general comments or suggestions you might have.

SERVICE CATALOG 🖥 105

Keep it simple and short. Automated surveys are okay to a point, but it's important to speak directly to customers when possible. This will provide more context and more insight than an automated survey. This "personal touch" directly with customers in the days and weeks following the launch is a world-class behavior. Make this a priority.

Figure 6.1 shows a close connection and feedback channels between the launch event and the update model. This connection and feedback occur immediately following the launch, and a reminder the update model must be defined and ready to engage before the launch. Any plan that assumes the update process can be sorted out after the launch is fundamentally flawed and will result in delays, customer frustration, and a poor initial impression of the Service Catalog which will be very difficult to overcome. On the positive side of this, a well-orchestrated launch with a ready-to-go update model complemented by a proactive customer outreach is likely to result in a great initial experience for customers that will set the right tone for the future.

> *With big wins in business today being elusive, the success of the Service Catalog is a bona fide game changer that brings value to both IT and the broader business.*

KEY INTEGRATIONS AND PARTNERSHIPS FOR SERVICE CATALOG

1. Service Portfolio: coordination and the business assessment that yield both the Service Catalog strategy and the Service Catalog scope.
2. Service Level Management: to participate in the

coordination along with the Service Portfolio Manager in the definition of the scope of the Service Catalog as well as to confirm the level of service and SLAs for each service in the catalog.

3. Service Requests: the Service Request Managers will be essential in providing the details for the service requests in the catalog and the fulfillment and workflow process. This is the "How" of the delivery of service.

4. IT Leadership: as a strategic initiative, the launch of the Service Catalog will have visibility with the CIO, VPs of IT, and most of the IT leadership team. The strategy, scope, and launch plan should be reviewed and discussed with IT leadership to get feedback and ensure the Service Catalog owners are in lock-step with IT leadership and there are no surprises later.

5. Non-IT Business Owners: partner with business leaders in HR, facilities, marketing, finance, and corporate shared services to design and develop the business services in the catalog that go far beyond IT.

TIPS FOR A SUCCESSFUL SERVICE CATALOG

1. Start with a Service Catalog strategy, as this will be a valuable reference throughout the design, launch, and operations of the catalog. Although this step is sometimes bypassed in the interest of time, it is a time and resource saver over time and sets the right course from the beginning.

2. Be focused on the business dependencies and the details of the fulfillment process for every service request in the catalog. This is a key to the success of

the catalog and in many ways the real heavy lifting of the catalog delivering value to the business.

3. A great Service Catalog will have a great front-end experience. It must be easy to use, fast, convenient, and personal. This is the first impression for the customer, and it must be a thoughtful and creative design effort.

4. It is likely that more Service Catalogs have failed due to an overly ambitious set of services at the outset than for any other single reason. Take a phased approach and start with a limited set of services to create a foundation of success. It is much easier to add services later than to pull back on a catalog that started too big and too complex.

5. Utilize a pilot period with user participation prior to the go-live of the catalog. This will drive out most initial problems and significantly reduce risk at the time of launch.

6. Know how you will keep the catalog current and accurate before going live. If the catalog is not accurate and loses credibility in the early stages, it is very difficult to earn it back.

7. Understand and appreciate the Service Catalog is very much "for the business" and not just for IT. Reach out to business owners across the organization and welcome the inclusion of non-IT service requests. Never underestimate the attraction of Service Catalog, and plan as well as design for flexibility and scalability from Day 1. You will be glad you did!

CHAPTER 7

PROBLEM MANAGEMENT

One of our Core 6 elements, Problem Management, is vital to every strong Service Desk and to world-class IT Service Management. Problem Management asks the question "Why," which puts us on the path to understanding incidents and problems and then on to their prevention. A mind-set of prevention is then the first step toward what will be the future model for IT—Proactive IT Service Management. More on that later.

WHAT IT IS

A problem is the cause of one or more incidents, and Problem Management facilitates the broader set of activities to first identify and then find a solution that will prevent the future occurrence of both incidents and problems. In the special case of incidents that cannot be prevented, Problem Management works to ensure the impact of these incidents is contained and minimized.

WHY IT IS IMPORTANT

Problem Management is a cross-functional process that works closely with the Incident Management, Change Management, and Release Management teams with a common goal of improving the quality of service. As problems are resolved the organization is the benefactor of preventing future incidents, which in turn reduces disruptions to the business, allowing the organization to perform at a higher level every day.

The most advanced organizations focus on proactive Problem Management activities which strive to resolve problems before incidents occur. Let's think about that for a moment.

> *Prevention is a very powerful model and a world-class behavior. Few things have the potential to change the world of IT, and prevention is one of the few.*

Simply reacting to incidents when they occur is of course necessary, but in this model we are not investing in the future; we are not protecting our future. We are simply reacting with what is an immediate and tactical pain point. This is survival, and that is not good enough.

Some key benefits of Problem Management include:

1. Prevention of future incidents and problems.
2. Elimination of recurring incidents.
3. Reduced disruptions to the business.

4. Collaboration with Incident Management and Change Management improves service reliability and quality.
5. Accelerated resolution of incidents.
6. Systematic reduction in the volume of incidents.
7. A greater understanding of risks to service delivery.
8. More effective workarounds for reducing incident impact.
9. Creation and improved utilization of the known error database.
10. Creates a culture of investigation and root cause analysis.

HOW IT WORKS

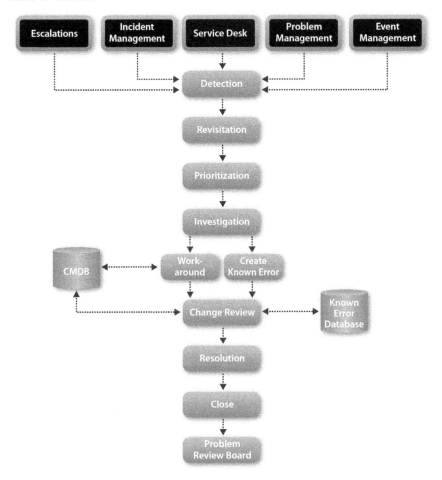

Figure 7.1 The Problem Management Process

Detection

The detection of a problem can come from a number of sources. In Figure 7.1 we have highlighted a few of these, including the Service Desk, Incident Management, Problem Management, and Event Management. While the detection and identification of a problem is becoming more sophisticated and aided by automation, there remains a level of judgment and experience necessary to raise a problem.

It's important to remember that a problem is the cause of one or more incidents and as a result it is necessary to look beyond a simple incident, and look at the patterns of incidents and their relationships. Technology has improved significantly in the past decade and can provide some assistance in the process, for example with Event Management providing early visibility of potential problems,

but there remains an important element of experience and judgment in this process.

This comes from our people in making decisions to investigate incidents and their causes.

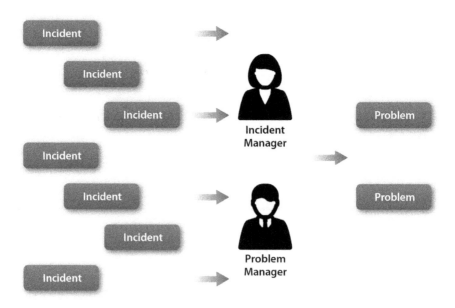

Figure 7.2 Incidents to Problems

Problem Management will work with the Service Desk and Incident Management to evaluate and identify incidents that can indicate a problem exists. This is not a simple evaluation; experience is very helpful and in some cases it can be priceless. Incidents can occur over time and ultimately be completely unrelated. Then, a single group of incidents can occur that are related and caused by a problem.

This fundamental cause-and-effect model then yields one or more problem registrations. This relationship is empirical and can't be modeled by any analytical means and so we rely on the knowledge, experience and investigation of the Problem Management and Incident Management teams.

> ### *This is one of the most important human elements in all of IT Service Management*

and virtually every world-class Service Desk has a strong Problem Management practice.

The details of how these companies practice Problem Management vary, but what the best organizations have in common are the following:

1. Problem Management is a priority.
2. Problem Management is staffed by experienced and knowledgeable people.
3. Problem Management metrics are tracked and published.
4. The culture is aggressive about registering and resolving problems.

Registration

When a problem is identified, it should be registered immediately so we can avoid any delays in the race to a resolution. Problems take a toll on our business, and it is important to resolve them quickly. This is another example of why speed is so fundamental to our standard of world-class.

Speed does not only apply to the speed of delivering a service, although this is always a good example—we want to make customers happy, and a fast response to a service request is a great way to accomplish this. But there is another important and very powerful dimension of speed and that is the velocity with which we address problems (and other issues in the business) and thereby minimize the impact they have on the organization.

Back to the topic at hand, registration of the problem. We need to capture a profile of what is known so our Problem Manager and team can take action. A typical problem record would look something like this:

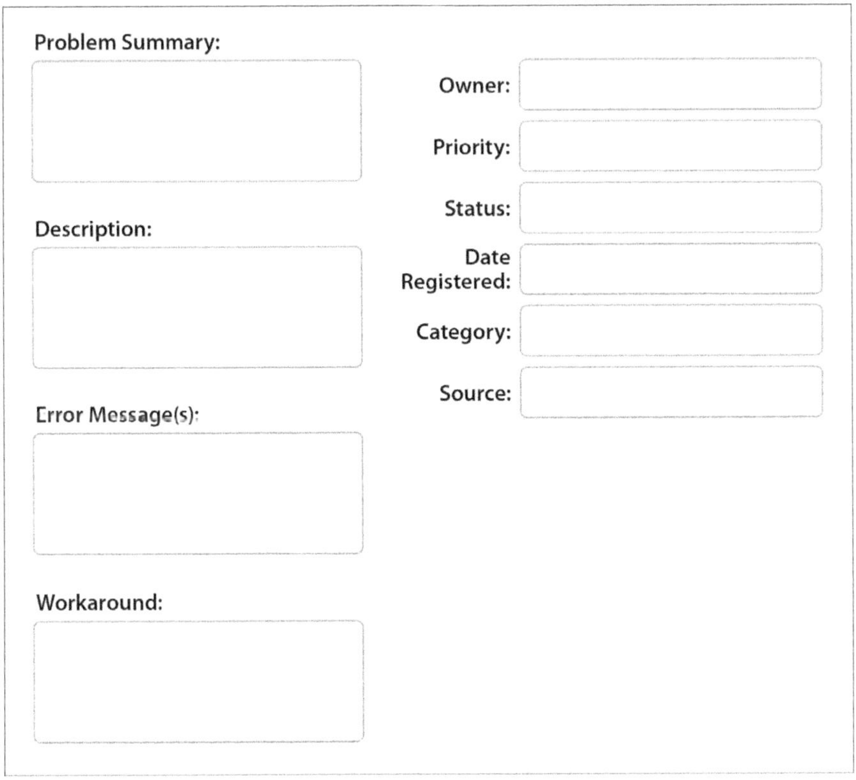

Problem Summary:

Owner:

Priority:

Status:

Description:

Date Registered:

Category:

Source:

Error Message(s):

Workaround:

Figure 7.3 Example Problem Form

The problem record will vary from organization to organization depending on the nature of the business and the nuances of the specific Problem Management process, but Figure 7.3 shows examples of typical fields that will provide an initial profile and allow action to begin immediately. The problem record will also provide information to support reporting and analytics requirements throughout the lifecycle of the problem and will also be used to complete historical analysis. This helps to understand trends and develop improved test plans and service improvement plans.

Prioritization

Every problem must be prioritized, which gives us an important piece of information to help us manage the problem through its resolution cycle. All problems are inherently important because they are problems and represent a risk to the business.

But not all problems are created equal

and because decisions need to be made about assigning resources and making investments, we will repeatedly refer to the priority of the problem. A few things to consider when assigning a priority:

1. Impact to the business
2. Cost to resolve the problem
3. People required to resolve the problem
4. Risk of additional incidents occurring
5. Is there a known solution?
6. Length of timeline necessary to execute the resolution

These factors are reviewed along with others and a priority assigned with the owner, who in most cases will be a Problem Manager. This owner will then drive and coordinate the actions of the business until the problem is closed.

This coordination performed by the Problem Manager will include working closely with both Incident Management and Change Management. It is important we understand and then capture the relationship between incident(s) and the problem. Beyond the scope of the individual problem, we use this information to understand trends and to look at prevention and service improvement plans. In this context of prioritization, the Problem Manager will often discuss the priority with the Incident Manager to get another view. Along these lines, a category also is assigned, and in many cases our problem category will match up with what we assign to the incidents. This is another topic to be covered with Incident Management.

> *The dialogue with Change Management is a proactive evaluation of any change that might be necessary as part of the problem resolution.*

This helps both teams—it helps Problem Management in determining the best course of action to resolve the problem, and for Change Management it provides an early view of future changes and puts some context and structure to the Change Calendar. This coordination, focused on this critical task of Problem Management, is a world-class behavior.

Investigation

With the registration, prioritization, and categorization processes completed, we move immediately into investigation. Some of this work is done in a ramp-up fashion during registration as the collection of facts and the profiling of the problem will begin to offer clues about the problem and a possible cause. A benefit of moving quickly through the registration and prioritization stages is that we are able to make investigation our focus, and only then does a resolution become possible.

As the transition and investigation are under way, if a workaround is known it should be applied immediately. This will help reduce the impact of the problem to the business while the investigation continues. It is important to continue the standard root cause evaluation even with the workaround in place because our goal remains to find a permanent solution if one exists. If a workaround is applied, it should be noted in the problem record, as this will help us with testing, training, and reporting. If a workaround is not known at the time, we try to identify one during the investigation to both help with this current problem and with any future problems.

Workarounds are valuable, and in some cases remain in place permanently if a permanent solution can't be found, creates too much risk to implement, or is too costly.

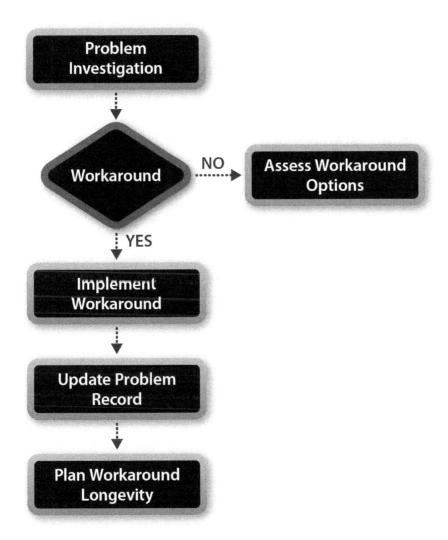

Figure 7.4 Problem Workaround Process

If a workaround is implemented, Incident Management and Change Management should be notified by the Problem Manager. This notification should include an estimate of how long the workaround is expected to be in place. This plan can change, but expectations should be set based on the best information available.

If a workaround is identified or, even better, a root cause solution, a known error record is created and applied to the known error database. This database is an important resource for Problem Management, for Incident Management, and for all of IT. It is referenced throughout the lifecycle of a problem and will be managed for quality and kept current by each Problem Manager.

As IT Service Management evolves in an organization and greater levels of maturity become possible,

> ***one model to take note of is moving beyond reactive Problem Management to proactive Problem Management.***

Reactive Problem Management is the standard—a process that starts with a reaction to incidents as they occur and creating problems and investigating problems only as the result of events that require it. Proactive Problem Management is a more strategic approach, a fundamentally different model in that our goal is to prevent incidents and problems before they occur. We can leverage a number of tools and techniques, including trend analysis, predictive models, and simulation tools. We can also perform What-If analysis in order to better understand the implications of a failure. This allows us to give more attention to an element of the infrastructure that represents a high risk and high impact.

> ***This in itself is not prevention, but the steps and analysis it enables are proactive and move us closer to prevention as a reality.***

In the chapter on Service Level Management (Chapter 9) we look at redundancy and resiliency—concepts that can be used in proactive Problem Management. For example, if we have experienced problems with a particular service on the first business day of each month and our trend analysis and simulations tell us another problem is likely to occur, we can implement redundancy for that service such that any failure in the future would allow the service to continue uninterrupted, utilizing the redundant service components. It is true that this is not prevention in the purest sense, but to the customer the failover is not visible and it is business as usual. This is all that really matters—the experience of the customer. While the redundancy is in place, our investigation should continue until a permanent solution is found for a problem that has not yet occurred but our analysis indicates is likely in the future.

As Figure 7.1 indicates, the investigation process and any change reviews will both rely on the CMDB as a source of information to provide the current and accurate view of incidents, problems, service requests, assets/CIs, and change requests to name a few objects that are relevant. Likewise, because Problem Management impacts many other processes, it is necessary to ensure the CMDB is updated as actions are taken throughout Problem Management.

> ***This includes relationships between incidents and problems, and problems with changes.***

In world-class Service Management we trust the CMDB, so

we manage it as a vital corporate resource. The Problem Manager must take ownership of upholding the quality of the CMDB.

A final comment on the investigation phase. In the case of problems that represent a high risk to the business and are resulting in recurring incidents, it can be necessary to escalate and deploy special skillsets across the organization. This process was described in the chapter on Incident Management (Chapter 4) and we can leverage the same model for Problem Management. Think of this as leveraging our best people to protect the business. I like to use incentives in these cases to reinforce the importance of a rapid solution to the problem, and to recognize and reward the talented people who possess the knowledge and skills to help solve important problems in the business. An escalation of this type is not a frequent occurrence, but when it is necessary, the visibility is very high as can be the cost to the organization if the problem continues.

> **So it makes sense to be aggressive and to rally our very best people around the problem.**

This is a trait of a healthy culture committed to improvement.

Change Review

Both workarounds and a permanent solution to a problem can require the implementation of one or more changes. This is another reminder that the Problem Manager must work closely with both Incident Management and Change Management throughout the lifecycle of a problem. Early visibility of changes driven by Problem Management improves communication across IT, and the Change Manager can assist the Problem Manager in defining the change request to avoid delays in evaluating the change.

If possible the Problem Manager should take advantage of scheduled CAB meetings to have any Problem Management-originated change requests reviewed and approved. The request should clearly state the relationship between the request for change and the problem. In the case of a major problem that is impacting the business, it might be necessary to implement an emergency change.

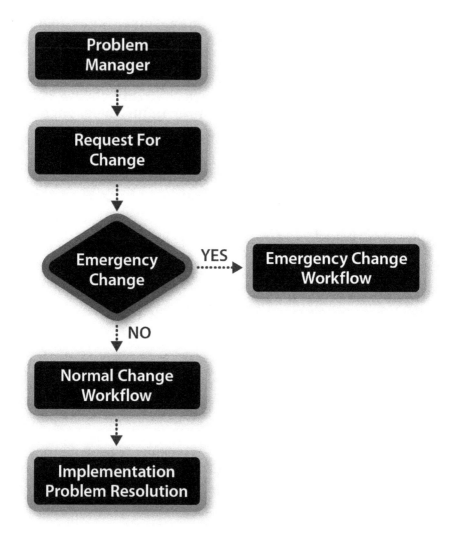

Figure 7.5 Emergency Change for Problem Management

The sponsorship and involvement of the Problem Manager will improve the communications in support of the change request and as a result improve the likelihood of an approval and the ability to move quickly into implementation. If necessary the emergency change process can be used to expedite implementation. It is important throughout this process that we preserve the relationships between incidents, the problem, and any changes. This allows all the teams working together to resolve problems along with IT management to better understand trends and to answer the question of "Why" we posed at the beginning of this chapter.

Resolution

With the cause of the problem identified, we can achieve a resolution—through a workaround or by way of a permanent solution. While always preferred, a permanent solution might not be understood, feasible, or practical. There are many complexities associated with the resolution, and we rely on the Problem Manager to navigate the organization through the process. In short, a permanent solution must be:

1. Well understood
2. Of acceptable risk
3. Affordable
4. Completed in a reasonable amount of time
5. Achievable with readily available skills
6. Measurably of more value than the best available workaround

As you can see the decision regarding final resolution is not a simple one. In some cases, workarounds can make a lot of sense and offer the best path forward. This is an example of valuable judgment offered by the Problem Manager and in consultation with the Service Desk and with Service

Level Management, Incident Management, and Change Management. As we did with a permanent solution, it is helpful to look at the profile of an acceptable workaround, which should be:

1. Stable
2. Low risk
3. Low cost
4. Achievable with current IT skills
5. A working solution for a reasonable amount of time
6. Understood and accepted by the customer or users

The final resolution, be it a permanent solution or a workaround, will be documented in the problem record and communicated to the affected teams. This communication is important, in particular for major problems, and should be managed and delivered by the Problem Manager. At this time any comments can be heard and recorded and any questions can be answered. This can help to support user acceptance and to avoid any confusion that could impact the Service Desk.

Close

As we near the end of our journey with an active problem, it is necessary to execute the final steps with some care.

When the problem is considered resolved, a cross-functional check is performed to confirm that any changes related to the problem are also completed and have been tested and verified. It is a good practice to get a confirmation directly from the Change Manager as further validation and to ensure there are no related issues—backing out the change for example.

In the interest of completeness, we should also resolve and close all the related incidents.

> *These relationships were important at the inception of the problem and are equally important as the lifecycle of the problem comes to an end.*

We don't have a complete record of the problem without these relationships nor do we have the information needed to do our best with trend analysis and other proactive Problem Management and related analysis. All these pieces must be documented and documented thoughtfully so we have a complete view of the problem and what occurred across the business.

With all these steps completed, and the related records updated, we can close the problem.

Problem Review Board

Regular problem reviews should be scheduled with the Problem Board if it exists, or convened with a cross-functional team that would include Incident Management, Change Management, Service Level Management, and other groups as necessary. This forum should also include members of IT Management.

It is common to suggest that these meetings focus on major

problems, but I like to see a broader view to include a summary of all problems, new types of problems, an update on problem trends, change metrics as related to changes opened to resolve problems, and major problems raised and closed since the last problem review. Because major problems represent a risk to the business, each should be reviewed to include the following points:

1. Major problem summary and date registered
2. Final resolution and date closed
3. Challenges encountered during the resolution process
4. Steps taken to mitigate the challenges in the future
5. Summary of follow-up actions

The volume and nature of problems in the organization will determine the frequency of problem reviews. Monthly or quarterly are most common, but if the business is seeing a surge in problems that are having a material impact, it might be necessary to convene more often for a period of time.

Ultimately the problem review process is about understanding and insight and taking proactive actions to prevent future problems and incidents, thereby protecting the future of the organization.

KEY INTEGRATIONS AND PARTNERSHIPS FOR PROBLEM MANAGEMENT

1. Incident Management: define relationships between a problem and the incidents caused by the problem.
2. Change Management: coordinate the request and

implementation of change(s) necessary to resolve a problem.

3. Service Level Management: investigation and assessment of problems and root causes that result in service failures.

4. Availability Management: evaluation of all problems impacting availability and joint planning to prevent availability issues in the future.

TIPS FOR SUCCESSFUL PROBLEM MANAGEMENT

1. Be clear in defining the relationships between incidents and problems as well as changes and problems from the registration of a problem through its closure.

2. Assign an owner to every problem and empower this role to work cross-functionally across the organization to keep the focus on a rapid resolution.

3. Measure and publish both incident and problem volume and resolution time metrics across the organization in order to create an understanding and a focus of improving these trends over time.

4. Have a plan, even if it is a long-term plan, to implement proactive Problem Management as a strategic investment to aid in the transformation to world-class.

5. Create a problem escalation model to reduce the time necessary to resolve high-impact problems and therefore mitigate risks. Utilize incentives to reward highly skilled people when problems are closed, and celebrate success.

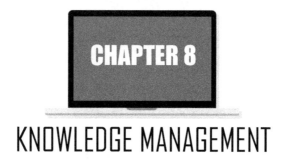

KNOWLEDGE MANAGEMENT

WHAT IT IS

Knowledge Management is the systematic collection, consolidation, and distribution of information in order to increase the quality and effectiveness of the Service Desk and all service and support channels.

WHY IT'S IMPORTANT

Knowledge holds tremendous value and can be leveraged across the full lifecycle of service delivery and by virtually every element of the organization. Benefits of Knowledge Management include:

1. More effective training of staff
2. Vastly involved incident and problem information
3. Enables a true knowledge transfer process

4. Accelerates the onboarding of new staff
5. Drives improved decision-making
6. Supports a higher quality service experience
7. Empowers the Service Desk team with the right information at the right time
8. Reduces the time required to close an incident or a service request, which translates to faster service delivery

HOW IT WORKS

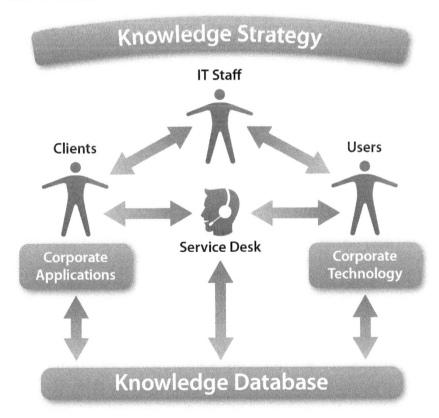

Figure 8.1 Overview of the Knowledge Management Process

Knowledge Strategy

An organization committed to ongoing improvement must have a Knowledge Management strategy. This can be simple in the beginning and evolve over time, but it must exist. This strategy recognizes the nature of knowledge and the value of this knowledge to the organization.

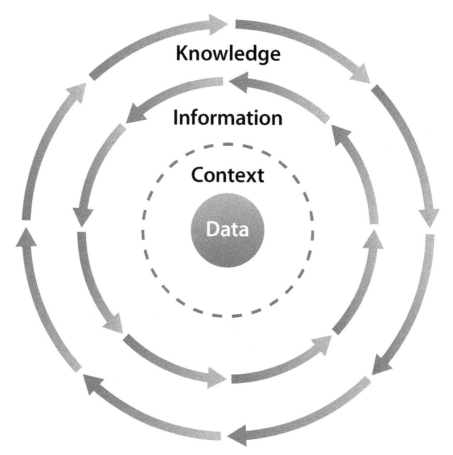

Figure 8.2 Knowledge Management Elements

Data provides us with the building blocks and with context. Data evolves into information, which in turn comes to life as knowledge.

The Knowledge Management strategy will define a number of important components:

 The Ultimate Goal of Knowledge Management in the Organization

 People Roles and Responsibilities

 The Technology Necessary to Support the Strategy

 Guidelines, Policies and Procedures to Govern Knowledge Management

 Key Performance Metrics, Milestones and Timelines if Needed

Figure 8.3 Knowledge Strategy Components

The roles and responsibilities definition must include organizational ownership for capturing, then communicating the Knowledge Management strategy. This should be seen as a desirable and high-profile assignment and one given to a talented person(s) in the organization.

Managing Information

From data grows information, and information is our bridge to knowledge. Context applied to data transforms endless units of fact into useful information that can be leveraged by people to do their job better and improve the quality of service.

Some planning is in order when creating a process to manage information. We need to understand:

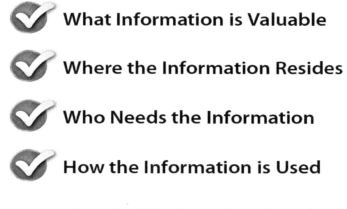

✓ **What Information is Valuable**

✓ **Where the Information Resides**

✓ **Who Needs the Information**

✓ **How the Information is Used**

✓ **How Do We Best Get the Information to the People That Need it**

Figure 8.4 A Process to Manage Information

With these points established, we can define a methodology to systematically collect the information, prepare it to be most useful, and deliver it to the people and teams in need of this fuel. Then, with experience and judgment, the information is transformed into knowledge and good decision-making.

> *This is a key output of the Knowledge Management process—better and faster decision-making.*

A world-class IT Service Management organization understands the value of information, nurtures this information, encourages all the people who are part of this process to enable the process, and provides constant reinforcement for the power of information.

The process must be understood by all, and for some organizations that have designated a "Knowledge Czar" or "Knowledge Mentor" in the organization, this role raises the visibility of Knowledge Management. This role can, among other things, communicate the information management process throughout the organization.

Knowledge Base

The knowledge base is a built-for-purpose database that supports the broader Knowledge Management initiative. I use the term *initiative* as Knowledge Management can have a broader role and broader visibility across the organization than other IT Service Management elements. We need to systematically hunt, find, and deliver the right information to the knowledge base.

This information can then be enriched and delivered to Service Desk staff, analysts, users and customers. This makes everybody better. A simple view of the knowledge base architecture:

Figure 8.5 Knowledge Base Architecture

The knowledge base is at the center of knowledge, and we leverage many diverse sources of information to populate, improve, refine, and enrich the knowledge base.

> *The knowledge base has the stature of a strategic and valuable asset to the business.*

The units of knowledge that live in the knowledge base, often called articles, are structured in a way that improves access and searching efficiency.

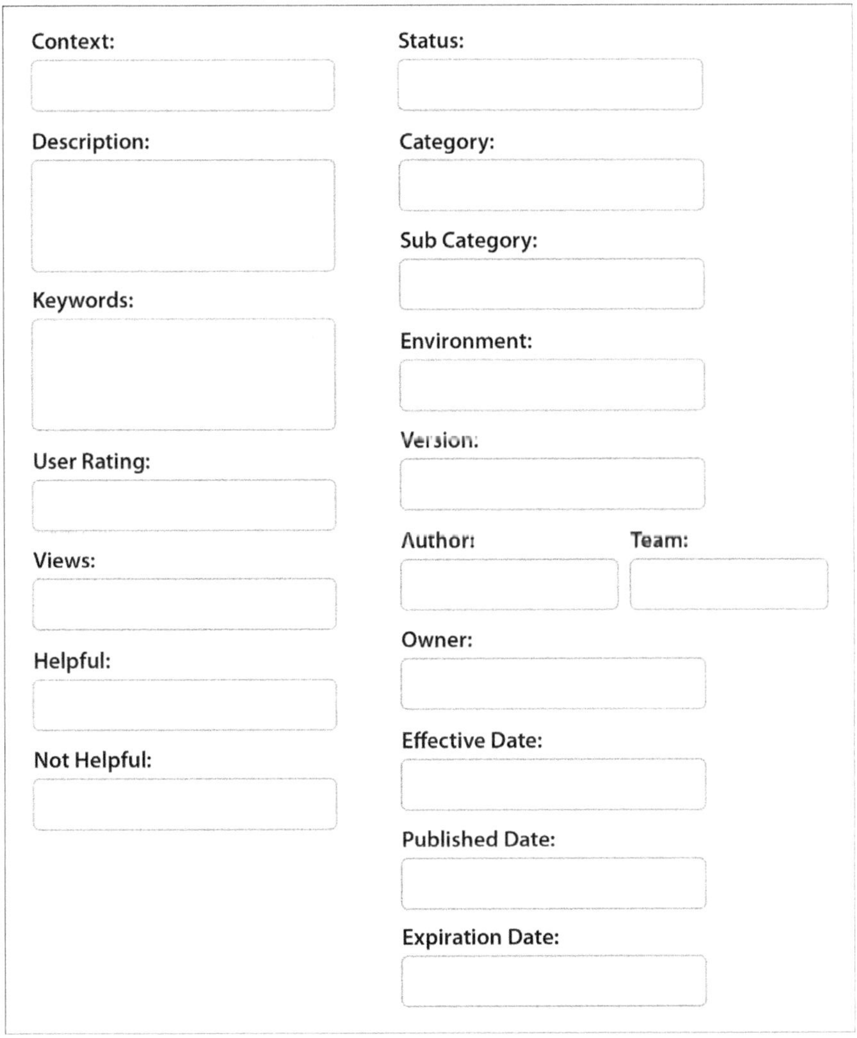

Context:

Status:

Description:

Category:

Sub Category:

Keywords:

Environment:

Version:

User Rating:

Author: Team:

Views:

Owner:

Helpful:

Effective Date:

Not Helpful:

Published Date:

Expiration Date:

Figure 8.6 Knowledge Article Structure

Information is stored in these templates, and shaped as needed based on the needs of the organization. Service Desk teams can conduct contests—a friendly competition— across teams with a goal to add the most knowledge items to the knowledge base. A month is a good time window, and a prize is presented to the winning team. This is fun, and brings attention to this important activity while accelerating the expansion of the knowledge base. This is good for everybody and can significantly improve the quality and scope of the knowledge base on an accelerated timeline.

Knowledge Transfer

Knowledge transfer is a dynamic process with people at the center. The effective transfer of knowledge poses a few key questions:

 Who are the Knowledge Experts?

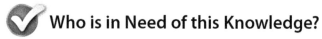 Who is in Need of this Knowledge?

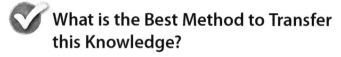 What is the Best Method to Transfer this Knowledge?

Figure 8.7 Knowledge Transfer

Different tools can be used to facilitate learning, tapping into the different learning attributes of people. Documents are effective for people with a high level of reading comprehension, but for others, written documentation is completely ineffective. Video technology has improved and can be a very productive learning tool. Yet another option is the live seminar.

These can be done in a creative and fun way, say over lunch or in a breakfast briefing.

A live seminar is interactive, and allows the knowledge expert to deliver the seminar in a real-time forum with discussion and Q&A. The key is using a good mix of these tools, keeping it fun and creative, and creating a knowledge transfer and communication plan to coordinate efforts and raise visibility across all teams.

KEY INTEGRATIONS AND PARTNERSHIPS FOR KNOWLEDGE MANAGEMENT

1. Incident Management: coordination on the offering of knowledge base access during the incident process. Should include who has access and the type of access provided.

2. Service Requests: determine and design the knowledge model and how it can complement the service request process. This will be different than Incident Management, so the right context is important here.

3. IT Management: the quality of the knowledge base will be driven by consistent and ongoing access to experts, and this must be supported and sponsored by IT leadership. It is certainly true that some knowledge articles can be created independent of the experts, but the diversity and depth of the knowledge base rely on business experts.

4. Service Catalog: design the right access model with the Service Catalog Managers for both internal user access to knowledge and the external customer access to knowledge. This recognizes the ascension of the catalog in the business, and as such, access to the knowledge base will occur as a complement to the Service Catalog.

5. Service Desk: a primary source of knowledge is the operation of the Service Desk and the daily volume of incidents and service requests, which can yield important knowledge articles to improve the speed and quality of service in the future. The process by which the right elements of knowledge make their way back to the knowledge base must be planned and executed in this partnership.

TIPS FOR SUCCESSFUL KNOWLEDGE MANAGEMENT

1. Take the time to create a Knowledge Management strategy and assign an individual or team to advocate the strategy.
2. Constantly reinforce that Knowledge Management is not about a database and collecting information—it is all about learning and making better decisions.
3. Identify, recognize, and reward your knowledge experts. These people are organizational treasures.
4. Set up a secure and scalable knowledge base. Set goals and incentives to drive the growth of the knowledge base quarterly and yearly.
5. Build a knowledge transfer plan and communicate it broadly. Leverage a mix of learning techniques that showcase the knowledge experts and nurture those learning. Make it fun. Keep it fresh.

SERVICE LEVEL MANAGEMENT

WHAT IT IS

Service Level Management defines and then works across the organization to ensure that all IT services meet or exceed the agreed-to standard while also developing a framework to govern the performance of all future services.

WHY IT IS IMPORTANT

Service Level Management represents all services across the business with the mission to both capture and communicate service level targets and to then monitor the day-to-day performance of these services.

When service level targets are not met, commonly referred to as a breach, Service Level Management will carefully evaluate the shortcomings of the service and develop a plan to prevent a similar breach from occurring in the future. At our best, we are looking beyond the scope of the current failure to understand trends or indicators that will help make us better prepared for the future.

Service Level Management provides a number of cross-functional and business benefits. Service Level Management:

1. Leads the process to define service level requirements and ultimately negotiates service level agreements for all services.
2. Expands the scope of managing to service targets to include operational level agreements (OLA) and underpinning contracts (UC) for all third-party suppliers.
3. Works to understand service failures and develop action plans to prevent future failures.
4. Serves as a business liaison to understand and communicate end-to-end service performance and the relationships and dependencies of all business functions.
5. Evaluates the quality of all services relative to SLAs, works to resolve disagreements between parties, and documents resolutions and any necessary revisions to SLAs.

HOW IT WORKS

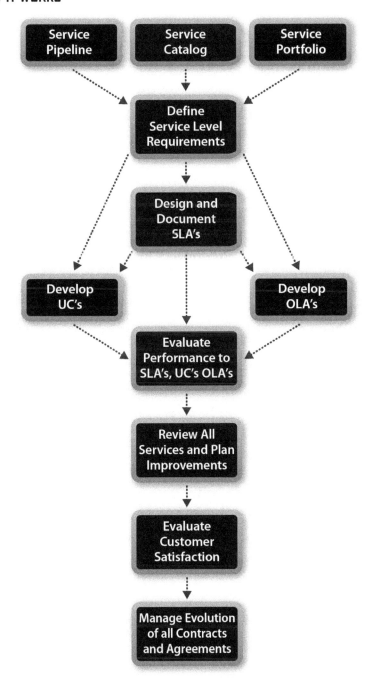

Figure 9.1 Service Level Management Process

Note: Throughout this chapter and others, I will use the terms *user* and *customer* interchangeably. You can make the argument that these are very different groups, but what is important in the context of IT Service Management is that we are delivering services to both, and the same principles and models apply in virtually every case. This is good enough for now, and any further treatment of the differences will wait for another day.

Define Service Level Requirements

Service Level Management is only possible with understanding—a real, in-depth understanding. There are no shortcuts. This only comes through working closely with customers and users of the service to review every element of the service, the primary use cases, the secondary use cases, and special use cases. A good place to begin these reviews is with a discussion of the business need the service is intended to satisfy. This can be a high-level discussion and provides the perfect context.

I want to take a moment to define the term *use case,* as it might not be familiar to some of you. A use case is an end-to-end description of a day in the life sequence of steps or actions that represent how a service is used by a customer in performing a necessary function.

> *Think of it as answering the question, "How do you use the service every day?"*

A written description is fine, but a storyboard is even better.

A storyboard uses a series of simple diagrams, flowcharts, and form mock-ups in combination with text to tell a story. Often, a whiteboard or paper flipchart are used; hence the term *storyboard*. This is an interactive, descriptive, and interesting way to both understand what users and customers need from the service and to build our use cases.

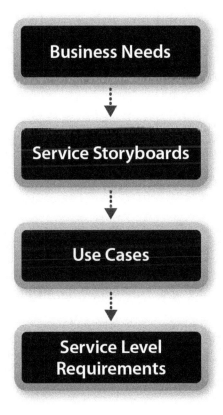

Figure 9.2 The Business Needs Hierarchy

With the context of the business needs overview, one or more storyboards to tell the story of the service, and a good set of use cases, we are now in a good and enlightened position to write the service level requirements. These are the detailed requirements that describe the performance of the service and the elements that will be addressed and ultimately quantified by the Service Level Agreement. The SLRs go hand in hand with the content and spirit of the SLAs.

Figure 9.1 shows the primary vehicles through which the services are developed and delivered to the business and to customers. There can be others, but the combination of the Services Pipeline, the Service Catalog, and the Service Portfolio provides a good view of the services, in early and later stages of their lifecycle, that will be addressed by the SLRs.

Design and Document SLAs

While the key to the SLRs is understanding the business need and the service we are delivering, the best way to describe the creation of Service Level Agreements is a negotiation. It's not easy, but it is absolutely necessary: We are attempting to craft the right balance of a few important factors, each of which has its own considerations and complexities.

The Level of Service Desired by the Customer

 The Level of Service IT is Capable of Delivering

 The Performance Elements to be Measured and the Metrics for Each

 The Cost Associated with Delivering the Desired Level of Service

Figure 9.3 The SLA Negotiation

The discussion and negotiation around each of these factors will take some time and likely several iterations. What we are trying to find is a level of service that is **acceptable** to the customer while at the same time being a level IT is **capable** of delivering and one the business is able to **afford**. Nobody will get exactly what they want, but everybody will accept a final SLA that we can all recognize as meeting the broader needs of the business, allowing us to operate a sustainable model every day.

This process is vital to the business. These SLAs, when written properly, put the business in a strong position every day by creating a happy customer who is consuming a level of service IT is able to achieve and which is within our budget.

***This is the essence of how we will operate
every day.***

Now, let's take this a step further.

In the course of negotiating the SLAs, we will naturally take a hard look at everything that is required to deliver the necessary levels of service. This will lead us to an understanding of the co-dependencies IT and the organization share, and further, on third-party partners and suppliers. We simply can't meet the SLA without the cooperation of and a commitment from these groups.

Figure 9.1 attempts to capture this extension of the SLA negotiations to include the third-party agreement, known as an underpinning contract or UC, and the agreements with another part of the same organization, known as operational level agreements or OLAs. These are good descriptive names that I mentioned briefly in the earlier section on benefits, but it bears repeating here.

The SLR and subsequent SLA discussions will normally lead the way and then extend into a preliminary framework for the UCs and OLAs and then finally detailed agreements that are in synch with the terms of the SLAs. After the first SLA iterations are completed, the subsequent drafts will incorporate the UCs and OLAs, because success is only possible if we take these on together. The Service Level Manager will lead this process, negotiate with all parties, own the contents of all agreements, and get the necessary approvals.

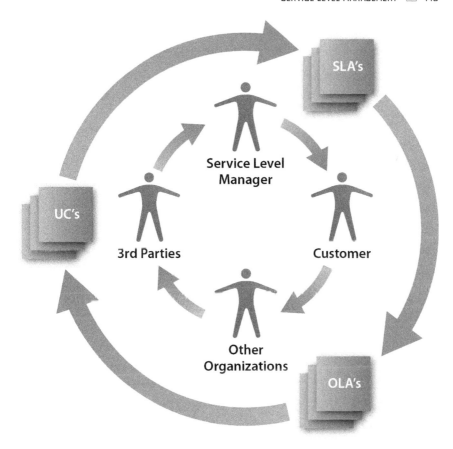

**Figure 9.4 The Broader Scope
of All Agreements & Contracts**

This cycle of dependencies, agreements, and cooperation is shown in Figure 9.4. Note that once jump-started by the Service Level Manager, this process is dynamic and never really stops, as we will see in the sections ahead.

When finalizing the SLAs, we can utilize a few different frameworks.

Service-Based SLAs address a single service for all

customers. This would apply to standard services with consistent requirements from customer to customer. A good example would be email—a well-understood service that is delivered to every customer. This type of agreement has the advantage of economies of scale, simplicity, and consistency.

Customer-Based SLAs address all the services consumed by a single customer. This would normally apply to larger or strategic customers where more customized SLAs make sense. This type of agreement can be personalized to the customer and address unique requirements where necessary. It can be used to reinforce a partnership model for the right customer type.

Combination SLAs address cases where a Service-Based SLA and a Customer-Based SLA are not the right fit. The Combination SLA does exactly what the name implies; it allows us to mix service, customer, and company level considerations in an agreement that will provide a hierarchical operating model, a flexible model where it makes sense, along with a customer and service specific model where needed. The Combination SLAs put more design work back on the Service Level Manager to create an agreement that captures the factors appropriately and in a way that is not overly complex, recognizing we will be operating under the agreement every day and reporting on how we are performing.

Evaluate Performance to SLAs

With experience in business we come to appreciate the truth in three simple management axioms:

We Cannot Manage What We Cannot Measure

 When We Begin to Measure Specific Performance, it is Likely to Improve

 When We Reward a Result, it is Likely to Occur and Then to Repeat

Figure 9.5 Essential Management Truths

What does this have to do with Service Level Management? Everything.

Everything we include in the SLA must be measurable. Put another way, if an item is under discussion to be included in the SLA but we can't reach agreement on how it will be measured, it should not be included. We spend a comparatively small amount of effort, although it certainly does not feel like it at the time, creating the SLA versus operating under its purview. The SLA will remain in place for the full lifecycle of the service, which can be many years. So, with the SLA in place, we turn our attention to how we are performing.

Although there will be a subjective element to answering this question, it is very much about clear and objective measurements.

The SLA will establish the specific metrics to be measured, and we can then agree to a report format and frequency with the customer so all involved know what to expect.

This should be as simple as possible. For example, if a service provider is delivering a cloud-based service, our SLA is likely to include a metric on availability. Let's assume both the monthly and the quarterly availability will be measured and that no single month can drop below 99.75 percent and no single quarter can drop below 99.85 percent. If we breach either of these numbers, service credits will be paid, and if we breach two or more quarters in a twelve-month period, a cash penalty will be paid on top of the service credit.

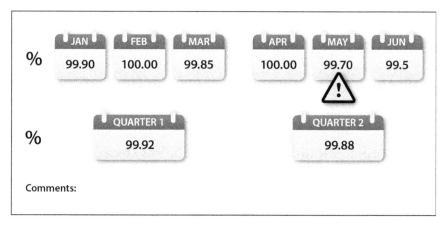

Figure 9.6 SLA for Availability of Service

Figure 9.6 shows an example of a simple availability report that can be published on a schedule all parties agree to. Normally, we want to see these weekly or every two weeks, and they will show a running total current up to the date the report is published.

Note the month of May breached the monthly availability metrics, and it is highlighted as a result. In spite of the month period breach, the quarterly metric was met. This availability report would include some explanation of the May breach in the comments field and should give some insight into what is being done to prevent future problems.

This availability report is easy to review, can be one panel on a single page that includes two or three metrics, and is part of a package that covers all SLA items.

The UC and OLA metrics should be added to the SLA report, and normally these metrics are fewer than what is covered by the core SLA elements. The format and approach should be the same.

Review All Services and Plan Improvements

As we are watching and measuring performance and delivering our reports and updates, the team is constantly on the watch for ways to improve. This can be both reactive—when a breach occurs, it is investigated to determine how we can prevent a similar breach in the future—and proactive—how we can make changes and investments today to address areas of risk and to get ahead of breaches before they occur.

It is necessary to do both.

We learn so much from a failure, and we need to take full advantage of each of these events to get better.

At the same time, reactive improvements are not enough, and this is certainly not a world-class model. Prevention gives us far more leverage than responding to problems. When there is a failure, the Service Level Manager coordinates the investigation with Problem Management, Incident Management, and Change Management.

As possible improvements are identified, they can be communicated in three different ways. Initial ideas can be included in the regular SLA report; improvements can be discussed and reviewed in more detail at regular service reviews; and any improvements that are approved and will be implemented should be documented in a service improvement plan (SIP).

Figure 9.7 Service Improvement Planning

Publishing SLA evaluation reports is helpful, but not enough. A good process to follow is a regularly scheduled service review. These are normally done quarterly, or twice per year. When a service is young, more frequent reviews can be necessary and useful to all parties. For a more mature service, twice per year or yearly can be enough.

A service review agenda would look something like this:

 **Review of Actions from Previous Meeting**

 **Review of Performance to SLA Metrics**

 **Update on Any Breaches and Exceptions**

 **Overview of Any Planned Service Improvements**

 **Update on Additional Changes in Service**

 **Customer Feedback on Service Experience**

 **Assignment of Action Items**

Figure 9.8 Service Review Agenda

The service review is a good opportunity to discuss any item that needs attention related to the service. Planned improvements should be presented and discussed: This includes a summary of how the customer experience will improve and any risks associated with the improvement. In some cases the customer may raise issues not considered by IT, and the plan can be adjusted accordingly. It is also a good time to get feedback from the customer on their overall service experience.

A good practice in these reviews is to ask the customer for specific examples of what they like most about the service, plus examples of what they dislike and any thoughts on how the dislikes can be addressed.

> *This is a time to listen carefully. Most customers will be very honest and give great feedback that can help us get better.*

These live discussions are helpful because customers will share information that might not come out in a survey or a short phone call. This feedback and the surrounding discussion can then be captured in the next update to the SIP. This plan is the single source of planned improvements and related information and is a living document for the full lifecycle of the service and owned by the Service Level Manager.

Evaluate Customer Satisfaction

The expectations of our customer take shape in the first step of our process—the definition of service level requirements. This early work is important because we need to recognize the connection between these early expectations: what will ultimately be documented in the SLAs, and our ability to meet these expectations and metrics throughout the lifecycle of the service.

If we set the wrong expectations or accept SLA metrics that will be problematic for us to meet,

we are laying the groundwork for an unhappy customer.

And an unhappy customer will require an investment of time and resources at a later time to turn them into a happy customer. This is bad for everybody. It is far better to carefully manage expectations from day one, to communicate clearly and often, and to craft metrics and a surrounding SLA the customer is happy with and we are confident IT can deliver.

This lays the groundwork for a happy customer, a happy IT staff, and a good partnership.

This is good for everybody.

We emphasize these points because our pursuit of a happy customer is all about getting off to a good start. Now, with our work done on the SLRs, SLAs, UCs, and OLAs, an operating service in place and our review of all services functioning, we need to seek and collect customer feedback early and often. Further, this process should use a mix of formal and informal channels, scheduled review and feedback review and feedback forums, and unscheduled and impromptu "how are we doing" checkups.

Throughout these discussions with the customer, it is important to have real data available on the performance of the service. Oftentimes, we will agree with the customer on the key performance attributes, but there will be times when perception does not match what the data shows. In these cases, it is valuable for IT and the Service Level Manager to have the latest data available so we can properly ground and guide the conversation if needed.

> *We are trying to create a 360-degree view of customer sentiment that will provide us with a real, accurate, and up-to-date snapshot of satisfaction.*

We can't fix a problem or concern we don't know about, so it's key that we get visibility of issues as quickly as possible. A few tools and techniques that can improve our visibility and keep the feedback fresh:

 Regular Surveys

 Scheduled Service Reviews

 Unscheduled Phone Calls to Get Top of Mind Feedback

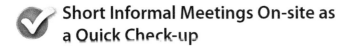 Short Informal Meetings On-site as a Quick Check-up

 Email Follow-up to Phone Calls or Meetings

 Customer Appreciation Events, Conferences and Networking Forums

 Customer Reference Programs and Awards

Figure 9.9 Staying Close to the Customer

It is not necessary to do all these things, but rather to pick a mix that makes sense for your business model and the service being delivered.

The key is frequency and consistency. We are building a relationship that leads to a successful partnership and, in turn, a happy customer.

One final comment: It is inevitable that we will face problems and disappointment with any service that is delivered over a period of time. How you respond to, communicate, and follow up at these times says everything about your organization. This is an opportunity to strengthen the partnership, and business people understand that problems will occur.

In these cases I strongly recommend a simple strategy. Contact your customer immediately, deal only in facts, take full responsibility, and tell them you are committed to doing whatever it takes to make things right.

Then, do exactly what you said you would.

This is world-class, and nothing less will do.

Manage Evolution of All Contracts/Agreements

Over time all businesses change, and we should expect the needs of our customers to evolve. Along with these evolving needs, so will the service need to adapt. However, there should be no surprises. Regular communications and discussions at the service reviews will provide early visibility of new business needs and any corresponding changes to a service.

Although changes will be necessary, all contemplated service changes must be carefully vetted to ensure the following:

The Investment Will Have a Reasonable Lifecycle of Usefulness

 Additional Changes to the Same Area are Unlikely in the Short Term

 It Will Improve the Value of the Service

 We Can Define a New or Updated Metric in the SLA

Figure 9.10 Evaluation of Changes to a Service

Of course, this is a simplification of the evaluation process, and the full analysis should be thoughtful and detailed. If we do determine that a change to an existing service is necessary, updates to the SLAs, UCs, and OLAs must be implemented at the same time. We should not let the service itself and the corresponding contracts and agreements get out of synch. It is not convenient but it is another organizational discipline we need to enforce. This is another world-class behavior.

A good process to follow is to draft any and all changes to the SLA, UCs, and OLAs and then convene a service review. The Service Level Manager can walk through all the updates to get agreement from all parties and to make any necessary final adjustments to the language and numbers.

> *This process presents a good opportunity to do a general document and contract cleanup, as we have all the right people at the table,*

and we should have a 100 percent current and accurate set of agreements when this revision cycle is concluded. The Service Level Manager will then issue the updated agreements to all stakeholders and update all plans of record to reflect the new baseline.

KEY INTEGRATIONS AND PARTNERSHIPS FOR SLM

1. Problem Management: work closely together on the investigation and analysis of all service failures and root cause analysis.
2. Service Portfolios: coordination of SLRs and SLAs for all new and existing services.
3. Service Catalog: coordination of SLAs and SLA changes for current services.
4. Service Pipeline: screening and SLR framework creation for all new services.
5. Change Management: review and liaison for all scheduled changes to services.

TIPS FOR SUCCESSFUL SERVICE LEVEL MANAGEMENT

1. Recognize Service Level Management as a key link in managing customer expectations and hence customer satisfaction throughout the lifecycle of a service.
2. Service Level Managers are customer facing and serve as a liaison across the business. This is a

decision-making role and as such must be empowered accordingly.

3. Manage the scope of the SLAs carefully. Avoid too
many metrics, and each must be measurable in a
clear and consistent manner.

4. Invest in high-quality Service Level Requirements.
This takes time, but poor SLRs will yield poor SLAs.

5. Leverage the Service Level Manager to build a strong
partnership with users and customers. This is based
on frequent, open, and honest communication
Celebrate success and overcome challenges together.

6. Take time to identify the key personnel who will
both enable the delivery of the service and the individuals to be consuming the service. This will provide a strong baseline for the delivery of the service
and a clear understanding of how the service will be
of value every day. We are looking for the real stakeholders in the broader process.

ASSET AND CONFIGURATION MANAGEMENT

Asset and Configuration Management is a strategic process and clearly a member of our Core 6. Configuration is a key, perhaps *the* key to a transformation from traditional Service Desk to IT Service Management. Asset and Configuration Management is also one of our most centric processes and maintains a close and dynamic relationship with both Change Management and Release Management. Looking a bit further, it is also logically linked with Incident Management, Problem Management, Availability Management, and Service Level Management. As Service Levels are closely tied to the experiences of users and customers, it is important to understand this dependency between service assets and the level of service performance they must enable to meet our service commitments.

WHAT IT IS

The management of IT Assets and Configurations

establishes the relationship between a service and the service components required to deliver the service to users and customers. All assets that are necessary to support the lifecycle of the service should fall within the scope of Asset and Configuration Management. These relationships enable the creation of a full logical model of the infrastructure of IT and to identify each configuration item (CI) that enables the operation of a service.

WHY IT IS IMPORTANT

The beginning of Asset and Configuration Management is the identification and definition of all service assets. This is often called an Asset Inventory, and building this inventory is itself valuable to an organization. It is not uncommon for the organization to have a poor understanding of what assets are owned, where they are located, and what employees are responsible for each asset. With the definition of the Asset Inventory, it is possible to create an accurate baseline and protect the integrity of all service assets and CIs going forward.

Asset and Configuration Management offers a number of benefits, including:

1. Improved understanding of the IT infrastructure.
2. The definition of the important relationship between each service and the CIs that enable the successful delivery of the service.
3. More effective coordination and planning of releases and changes.
4. Preserving the integrity of IT assets and the IT infrastructure.

5. The creation of a central database that provides a current and accurate definition of all IT components, assets, and CIs. The physical database is often referred to as the configuration management database, or CMDB. There can be multiple CMDBs that are part of a multilayer configuration management system (CMS).

6. Asset and Configuration Management improves the understanding of incidents and problems and reduces their resolution times.

7. Effective Configuration Management is necessary to meet the requirements of fiscal, audit, governance, and compliance.

8. Is truly transformational to the understanding an organization has of how services are delivered and the ability of management to perform impact analysis and conduct scenario planning.

9. Asset and Configuration Management enables strategic and investment planning in support of critical business services.

10. The CMS and CMDB can provide the most complete and accurate view of the complete IT estate and provide the opportunity to create a federated data model in support of the business. This in turn is a critical element to successful audit and compliance activities.

HOW IT WORKS

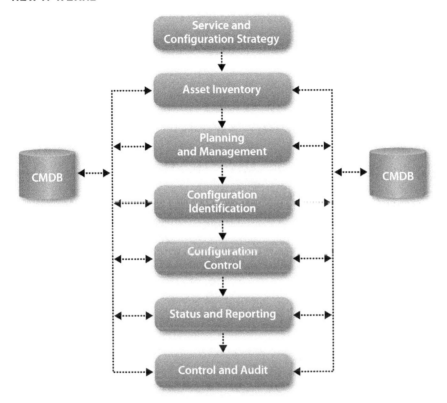

**Figure 10.1 Asset and
Configuration Management Overview**

The Asset and Configuration Management process is foundational to virtually every part of the organization. In many ways it is the essence of IT in that it ensures well-managed and healthy IT assets and service components, each of which in turn supports the day-to-day performance of all people, enabling the organization to be at its collective best in delivering products and services to its customers.

A strong Asset and Configuration Management process is likely to result in healthy and high-performing assets and CIs that in turn enable high-quality services.

Conversely, a nonexistent or weak Asset and Configuration Management process is likely to result in unreliable and low-performing Assets and CIs that leave the full organization poorly equipped to deliver services, and this results in frustrated employees and unhappy customers. These linkages are inevitable. Good begets good and bad begets bad. So, we need to get Asset and Configuration Management right. It is central to our Core 6 and to world-class IT Service Management.

Service and Configuration Strategy

Asset and Configuration Management is most effective when performed in the context of a Service and Configuration strategy that brings together the full portfolio of services to be offered, with the baseline of all components that enable the delivery of service and products. If we simply build an inventory of assets and components without this service strategy, it is very difficult to both effectively manage the Asset Inventory and make decisions on which Assets and components will be placed under the care of Configuration Management. These items are in turn referred to as the Configuration Items we described earlier.

It should be noted that not all assets and service components will be designated as CIs. This is necessary for two reasons. First, CIs should be those assets or components that directly enable core or strategic services to be delivered and as a result are most critical to the business; they should be managed to ensure reliable performance, high availability, and an optimal lifecycle of usage in the organization. Second, the sheer number of assets in many organizations is simply too large to be put into the Configuration Management process. It is not uncommon for this number to reach into the tens of thousands; this becomes unmanageable and reduces the effectiveness of the asset and Configuration Management process overall. And not focusing on the right assets greatly reduces the value of what should be a high-value process.

The Service and Configuration Strategy can help answer the question of which assets and service components should be designated as CIs and ensure these CIs are then directly in support of core services, new services to be launched, and the broader business strategy.

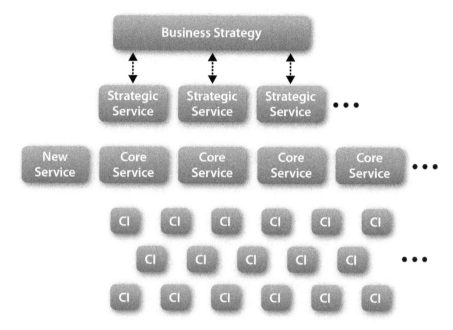

Figure 10.2 The Business Strategy Hierarchy

The strategy also provides a logical and physical model that puts our focus on the assets that really drive the business.

Asset Inventory

The early steps of Asset and Configuration Management must include a complete discovery of all Assets currently deployed in the organization. It is true that too often an enterprise does not accurately understand how many assets exist, where they are, and what they are. Good tools exist today that can automate this process, quickly identify all assets on the network, and return a profile of attributes for each asset.

This is a good beginning and provides an accurate and starting baseline.

If this has not been done previously, or it has been a while since this information was updated, there will likely be some surprises.

But the facts are the facts, and with this information we can move forward. Each asset, some to be designated as CIs, will be profiled by a number of descriptive attributes. These fields will be determined by the type of asset. For example, a desktop computer would look something like this:

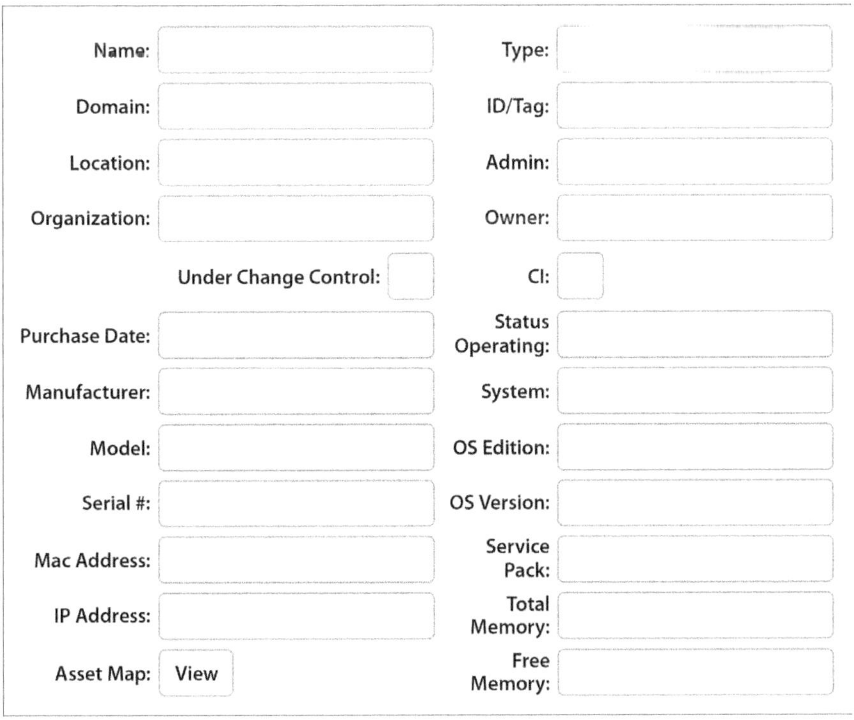

Name:		Type:	
Domain:		ID/Tag:	
Location:		Admin:	
Organization:		Owner:	
Under Change Control:		CI:	
Purchase Date:		Status Operating:	
Manufacturer:		System:	
Model:		OS Edition:	
Serial #:		OS Version:	
Mac Address:		Service Pack:	
IP Address:		Total Memory:	
Asset Map:	View	Free Memory:	

Figure 10.3 Example Asset Attributes

Each organization will determine how many resource types are necessary and what attributes and fields make sense for each asset type. This information will be held in a database to provide a helpful reference and to enable reporting and analysis.

Note that IT assets should not be assumed to be hardware only, these assets can also include software, facility assets, people, contracts, and documentation. In the early stages of Asset and Configuration Management, we want to keep things simple, stay focused on understanding the strategy and policies that will guide this process forward, and get some of the basic information in place quickly. To this end, the Asset Inventory can be created initially before the CMDB or CMS are in place. This simple step can very helpful to the organization and provide valuable visibility of assets that in many cases was lacking in the past. The Asset Inventory can be a simple table or collection of spreadsheets that then come under Configuration Management at a later time. This progression is practical and very common. The Configuration Management Database is necessary to a successful Asset and Configuration Management implementation, but it takes time to design and assemble the CMDB, so it will normally come together later in the process.

> *I often see organizations underestimate the time required to implement the CMDB as it touches so many elements of the organization. It is important to be patient.*

In most organizations there is another activity that occurs as Asset and Configuration Management is launched and the CMDB is under construction. This activity is the cleansing of existing IT information, asset databases, and other data sources inside and outside IT.

This can be a big undertaking and is part of the cultural shift necessary for IT Service Management. It is not un-usual to find that existing data is outdated, inaccurate, in-complete, or contains duplicates. These issues need to be addressed and reconciled in the run-up to creating the first version of the CMDB. This effort can be led by Configuration Managers; it is a cross-functional effort and one that is criti-cal to the success of the CMDB and Asset and Configuration Management.

Although Asset Management and Configuration Management are combined in this chapter and commonly in the model of IT Service Management, there are some dif-ferences between the two. **Asset Management** is focused on tracking the ownership, condition, and value of assets through an expected lifecycle. Asset Management has the perspective of a collection of individual assets.

Configuration Management has some fundamental dif-ferences from Asset Management. The focus shifts from assets that are simply assets to be identified and tracked, to assets that are necessary to deliver a service and a key distinction, the relationships between assets, the ser-vices they enable, and the customers who consume the services. These relationships create a logical model that then can be used to manage the full scope of IT Service Management.

The most advanced IT Service Management software

applications can capture this logical model in a graphical service map.

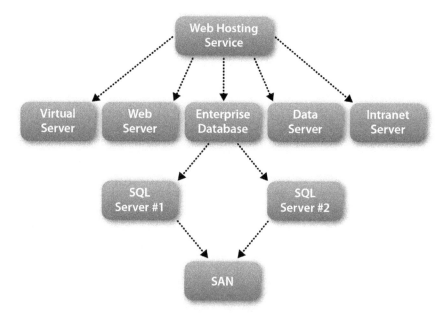

Figure 10.4 Configuration and Service Map

This service map and the logical model it represents provide a lot of useful information, and are far more descriptive than looking at a large table of fields and records.

This view can give us some guidance in the identification of CIs—if an asset is part of the logical model for the delivery of an IT or Enterprise Service, and therefore needs to be under the control of Change Management, it likely qualifies as a CI. We can then follow this approach to making good choices on what assets are simply assets and which assets are CIs.

Planning and Management

The strategic and cross-functional nature of Asset and Configuration Management dictates that we have a thoughtful plan that provides guidance to the organization on the approach, responsibilities, and details to be inherent to the Configuration Management process. This information is provided in a Configuration Management Plan to be developed and maintained by the Configuration Management team. This plan should include:

1. Objective and Summary
2. Critical Requirements
3. Policies
4. Roles and Responsibilities
5. Tools and Systems
6. Implementation Plan
7. Key Integrations
8. Communication and Metrics

The Configuration Management Plan is reviewed with IT Management and in some cases with Executive Leadership as it has implications across the business. Following approval, the plan is then distributed to all IT Service Management process owners, including Change Management, Release Management, Problem Management, and Service Portfolio Management. It is also important that a further coordination with the Service Level Management team is occurring during this process for visibility of the plan—which is good in itself, but also a critical view of the Configuration Management Plan from the perspective of service levels. Other teams can be included as needed, and it becomes clear that

> ***this plan and its contents influence virtu-
> ally all IT Service Management processes.***

This is ultimately a good thing as it provides a broad and holistic strategy to managing the IT infrastructure and mobilizing the assets of IT with an eye toward the relationship with delivering services. These relationships and linkage to the business are the lifeblood of the future of IT.

As we now move into the core elements of Asset and Configuration Management, Figure 10.1 shows the connection to and support provided by the CMDB. Some large organizations will implement a full Configuration Management System, but this is not always practical. What I see most often is the CMDB as the database of choice for Asset and Configuration Management information. This is a more practical and leaner model with the added benefit of being implemented more quickly. In most cases the CMDB will also hold incident, service request, problem, change, and release information along with all other objects and information associated with the full IT Service Management process lifecycle. This is a big value the CMDB can provide—serving the organization as the single source of asset, CI, services, and complete Service Management information for IT and for the broader organization.

Where a CMS does make sense, an overview of the model is shown in Figure 10.5:

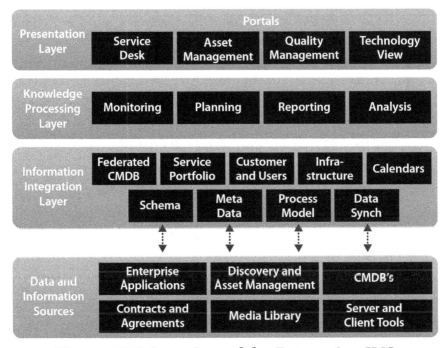

Figure 10.5 Overview of the Enterprise CMS

The representation of the CMS shown in Figure 10.5 provides some idea of the scope and complexity of implementing this model. This version has been simplified somewhat, so the reality would include additional elements in each of the four layers.

The standard practice of organizations today is to implement a CMDB as the Core 6 and additional processes are stood up. The next level of the evolution and scale would be a **Federated CMDB,** which is a model that includes multiple CMDBs reflecting some combination of multiple business units in a distributed enterprise as well as the database(s) of outsourced providers, partners, and suppliers. The Federated CMDB is able to provide a broad span of control and effective data integration.

For a further level of maturity and scalability, a CMS can be implemented that leverages the Federated CMDB as an element of the Information Integration layer and is normally best suited to large and distributed enterprises.

> *The CMS model requires careful planning and design and must be managed by a senior Configuration Manager or team of managers in the case of a large multinational organization.*

Configuration Identification

The effectiveness of Asset and Configuration Management is very much about accurate asset, CI, and relationship information. Configuration identification provides a naming convention along with a versioning scheme for all assets and CIs. This is extended to include the full set of attributes that will describe the item while providing the information that is actionable in the management process.

Configuration identification also helps with the selection of CIs and the hierarchy of any of the different CI types. Each CI will be assigned an owner, and a process-related decision must determine when a CI will be put under the control of Configuration Management. A decision can be made to designate an asset or service component as a CI, but the effective date for entering the Configuration Management process can be set to a logical date in the future. This could be aligned to the first day of a month, the first day of a quarter, or to combine a number of CIs into an onboarding bundle to avoid CIs coming into Configuration Management one at a time.

With an agreement in place on the naming convention and attributes for CIs, this should be captured in a document that is created and maintained by Configuration Management and distributed to the organization as a helpful reference. This information is especially helpful to the Change, Release, and Problem Managers. The definition element of configuration identification doesn't end with individual CIs and their attributes. The relationships we touched on earlier have a strategic importance in that they provide a more complete understanding of the CIs that have a relationship with other CIs, and the logical set of CIs that together enable the delivery of a service as well as enhancing the full and complete description of a service. This is fundamental to Service Level Management. These relationships are maintained in the CMDB along with the CI records and allow us to derive a graphical map like the one shown in Figure 10.4.

A hierarchy of CIs provides a rich language to capture relationships and the ability of CIs to support the business.

CI relationships can be One to Many; Many to One; and One to One as depicted in Figure 10.6.

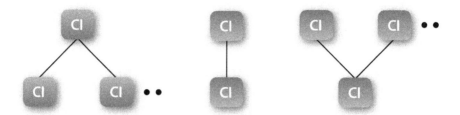

Figure 10.6 The CI Hierarchy

Beyond describing how CIs can work together to provide a service, relationships also describe the connections between CIs and incidents, problems, changes, and releases.

> *Thinking about this for a moment, you begin to have an appreciation for the associations that exist throughout our IT Service Management processes,*

the services we provide, and the assets, components, and CIs that together keep the organization and its people running every day.

Configuration Control

Configuration Control establishes the activities and procedures that govern the necessary control of CIs. When we begin to appreciate the importance of CIs to the business in that they together enable the delivery of every IT service and enterprise service, it is clear that we need to establish a comprehensive set of controls for these precious resources. Fundamentally, we need to define these core procedures:

1. Adding a new CI
2. Modifying an existing CI
3. Removing a CI

The *adding* and *removing* references are to the entry of a CI into the scope of Configuration Management and the exiting from the same process.

We do have a natural process that can be leveraged for item #2 above; Change Management provides what is necessary and when an asset qualifies to be identified as a CI. There is value that needs to be protected, and this value to the business is addressed through Change Management for the full lifecycle of the CI until such time as the asset is removed from Configuration Management. This removal can be the result of a change in status of the asset, a change in the use of the asset, or a decommission or retirement.

It is important to make a distinction between managing changes to CIs or Change Management, and the management of the configuration record, or Configuration Management. These two processes are closely related, depend on one another in order to be effective, but are not the same.

> *There is a context to Configuration Control,*
> *one that is provided by the type of CI and*
> *the services the CI enables.*

It is not possible to establish the right level and model for configuration control of each CI until this is understood. One size of configuration control does not fit every CI.

Configuration control is necessary to manage the activities against the configuration baseline. A configuration baseline is a specific configuration definition for a service or product that has been reviewed and approved as an anchor for all subsequent activities related to the configuration. Baselines can be very useful in rebuilding a specific version of a service or a product, to define a milestone in the evolution of a service, and to provide a back-out plan in the event of a failed change.

Status and Reporting

A key goal of Asset and Configuration Management is to maximize both the value and productive lifecycle of assets, service components, and CIs. For this to be possible, we must track and document CIs through each phase of their lifecycle. The number and types of stages will depend on the CI and will be fit for purpose by the Configuration Managers.

The status of the CI gives us insight into the current state of the asset, the history of the asset, and defined performance parameters. Think of this as a report card for the CI—what is it doing today and how is it performing? With the status and visibility data and tools in place, we can then create the reports needed to provide the insights to manage toward that goal of maximizing the value and useful lifecycle of the CI.

Typical configuration reports could include:

1. A list of all CIs

2. CI history summary
3. CI baseline history
4. CI change history
5. Unauthorized changes to CIs
6. 90-day new services summary
7. New CI summary
8. Retired CI overview

With current and accurate CI status information, we make a virtually endless variety of reports possible, and these reports can be shaped to the current needs of the organization.

> *We should not kid ourselves—creating reports based on inaccurate or outdated information is a waste of precious time.*

Seems obvious, but it is surprising how often this occurs when the focus should be first on getting the status information right.

Most if not all of the information needed will be living in the CMDB and the native database tool, or the ITSM software application can be used to generate the necessary reports. These tools have improved a great deal over the past decade and make it much easier to get access (including searching and analytics tools) to the data and reports we need.

> *This provides another reminder that we look to the CMDB or CMS if appropriate to be the single source of truth for IT information in the business.*

Control and Audit

Audit is a vital part of the complete Asset and Configuration Management process. This can and likely will include some level of Asset and Configuration Management-conducted internal audit along with audit conducted by outside parties in support of governance and compliance. Health care and financial services organizations are subject to the processes, and the requirements of audit and compliance are growing for many other markets as a complement to good corporate governance and stewardship.

As IT Service Management maturity grows, the Asset and Configuration Management team will conduct audits to verify that:

1. The current state of CIs matches the CMDB/CMS record.
2. Change, Release, and Configuration Management processes are documented and daily practices match the documentation.
3. Documented baselines match the current physical infrastructure.
4. New CIs, modifications to CIs, and retired CIs are immediately reflected in the CMDB/CMS.

A strong internal audit process conducted by the ACM team will benefit the business immediately in addition to better preparing the organization for any external audits and compliance efforts. World-class IT organizations set high standards for, and demand a great deal from, themselves, independent of any external requirements. This creates a cultural standard of excellence and accountability that improves virtually every aspect of Service Management and in turn establishes IT as a leader and influencer across the broader business.

A characteristic that is shared by world-class Service Management organizations is a commitment to being successful with audits and governance. In some cases the organization is great today, and in some cases there is a plan to be great.

> *This success takes time and is another journey within the journey, so what's important is the commitment—It all starts here.*

A few activities that can help with a successful audit:

1. Document, document, document—starting with documentation for each of the current primary IT Service Management processes in operation. I have seen great examples of an Incident Management handbook or a Change Management manual written by the process owners and used often across the organization.
2. Prepare reports on the major production rollouts of new software and new hardware into the production landscape.
3. Document all unauthorized changes, what happened, and steps taken to ensure the risk is addressed in the future.
4. Generate a report on the Change Success Rate and profile any failed changes.

5. Prepare a report on the process by which the testing and staging teams move changes and build into production.
6. Prepare a report on planned new services and the process used to roll out new services to the business.

There are of course many, many others, and in the case of audit preparation, less is not more. More is probably good and will provide us with thorough documentation and thoughtful reporting, along with critical analysis of failures and exceptions that are all necessary for success.

KEY INTEGRATIONS AND PARTNERSHIPS
FOR ASSET AND CONFIGURATION MANAGEMENT

1. Incident and Problem Management: evaluation and diagnosis of all incidents, major problems, and trending.
2. Availability Management: coordinated testing and risk management planning in support of required availability targets.
3. Change Management: validation of requests for change and coordination of planned changes and impact analysis activities.
4. Financial Management: cooperative work on business cases, cost analysis, and risk assessment.
5. Service Catalog/Service Portfolio: assessment of infrastructure and service component requirements associated with the introduction of new services and the retirement of existing services.
6. Service Level Management: close coordination of Configuration Planning activities and the

management of asset lifecycles to fully consider the implications to service levels and SLAs. These relationships are important but not always clear, so the trained eye of the Service Level Managers is much needed at the right time.

TIPS FOR SUCCESSFUL ASSET AND CONFIGURATION MANAGEMENT

1. Take steps to ensure a strategy is in place that provides guidance on the connection between services and infrastructure; how does our configuration enable the delivery of the Core Strategic Services.
2. Build an accurate inventory of asset information— this will require an investment of tools and time but will be well worth it. A good process operating with bad data will fail.
3. Relationships bring Configuration Management to life. Capture and then maintain the relationships between CIs and services, plus incidents with problems with changes and with CIs.
4. Make the Configuration Management Plan a required document and one that is regularly updated and delivered to the extended IT Service Management team, process owners, and business stakeholders.
5. Name owners for the Configuration Management process and empower them to enforce the necessary standards while holding the organization accountable. These individuals should be selected carefully and bring the right mix of experience, expertise, and communication skills. It is, and should be treated as, a key role in the business. A natural extension of this

same concept is the designation of asset stakeholders who bring a unique knowledge of specific strategic assets and provide the care that must be taken to ensure the asset is not marginalized.

6. Recognize that asset and configuration are key to audit and governance success. Establish a partnership between these teams from the beginning and take care to ensure audit, compliance, and governance requirements are reflected in both the Service and Configuration Strategy from Step 1 in Figure 10.1, and in the Configuration Management Plan. This influence becomes a natural part of the plan if included from the beginning but very difficult to add later as an afterthought.

CHAPTER 11

CHANGE MANAGEMENT

Each of the processes we review throughout the book is important and plays a vital role in world-class IT Service Management, and I have included each because they have repeatedly proven their value to real businesses. A few of these processes, however, are truly transformational. Change Management is one such process and has earned its place as one of our Core 6 elements.

It is certainly possible to operate a Service Desk, even a pretty good Service Desk, without having a Change Management process in place. However, I have not seen a world-class Service Desk that was missing Change Management. We will explore these reasons in more detail throughout the chapter, but in essence the lack of Change Management puts the organization at risk. It is a virtual certainty that unplanned outages will occur and create disruptions to the business and ultimately impact revenue and customer retention. It is also true that organizations with no Change Management process in place suffer a number of other symptoms that are not predictable but will always exist and impact the quality of service delivered. I often describe Change Management as a process that can take an organization "to the next level" of both performance and maturity, but this must come with the right level of organizational commitment.

WHAT IT IS

Change Management is a set of structured operating rules and processes that ensures all changes to a service or infrastructure are performed in a consistent manner that minimizes risks and maximizes value to the business.

WHY IT IS IMPORTANT

Always vital to Service Management, Change Management has assumed a more strategic role in the business today due to the growing complexity of IT infrastructure, the proliferation of mobile devices, increased accountabilities born of new audit requirements and government regulations, and the emergence of new security challenges. Effective Change Management offers compelling benefits.

1. Reduces unplanned outages
2. Faster recovery from service interruptions
3. Accelerated rollout of new service offerings
4. Fewer emergency changes
5. Creates accountability for unauthorized changes
6. Establishes a change calendar for the business
7. Reduces the number of failed changes

HOW IT WORKS

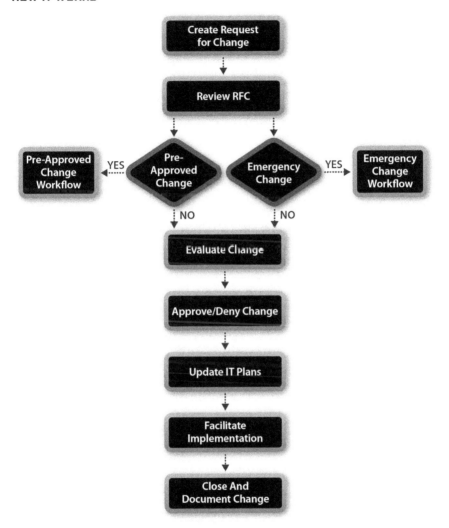

Figure 11.1 Change Management Overview

Create Request for Change

A change request is raised by an individual or group in the business and must contain the information necessary for the initial review to be completed. Care should be taken to ensure all information is included in order to avoid delays. The template for this request will vary from organization to organization, but some examples of the fields that should be included are:

Requester:

Change ID:

Date:

Location:

Email:

Phone:

Service:

Summary:

Resources:

Known Risks:

Benefits:

CAB Date:

Figure 11.2 Example Change Request Template

The request form should be as simple as possible while also including the information most important to the RFC review process. Errors in data input can be minimized by using assigned, pre-populated, and pull-down menu values. Some time should be taken to provide a meaningful **summary** of the request, an accounting of the **resources** that will be required, including for testing and implementation, any known **risks**, and a summary of the **benefits**.

A complete and thoughtful request will speed up the process and increase the chances of an approval. A poorly crafted request will slow down the process, cause the reviewer to come back to the requester for more information in many cases, and reduces the chances of an approval. An important element of Change Management is accountability, and the accountability begins with the request. Some world-class IT organizations are now tracking the approval and denial records of requesters to further enforce the accountability inherent in raising a request for change in the organization. As an interesting extension of this accountability model,

> *we now see some teams tracking the voting record of all CAB members, including how often they voted, when they did not vote, how quickly they voted, and how they voted.*

This information is then provided to the CIO and other members of IT senior leadership.

Review RFC

The Change Management process must be agile and designed to make good decisions quickly and consistently. In keeping with this spirit, the Review RFC step should be a quick initial review to consider the following:

1. Has the RFC template been completed properly?
2. Do the key fields provide the necessary detail?
3. Is the request sensible and within the scope of Change Management?
4. Is the RFC a duplicate of an existing request?
5. Is it necessary to return the RFC to the initiator for additional information or clarifications?
6. Is the overall nature of the RFC such that it will be denied at this initial review?

The initiator of the RFC should be notified of the results from the initial review immediately to allow a prompt response as appropriate. In some organizations an appeal of a denied request is permitted.

If the RFC qualifies to continue through the process, it is then determined if the request qualifies as a preapproved change or an emergency change. If so, the appropriate workflow is invoked. If not, the request continues to the Evaluate Change step as a **Normal Change**.

Preapproved Change

The preapproved Change workflow enables a greater focus on the significant changes that require a more rigorous evaluation. The preapproved change will represent a change that is low risk, low cost, and implemented with a minimum resource requirement. With this profile it is often the case that these changes also represent a high volume item and help to reduce the volume of requests moving into the Evaluate Change step.

In some cases, the preapproved change will require an approval from the initiator's manager in order to provide a simple but effective level of review. The change then moves to the implementation phase together with other CAB-approved changes.

Figure 11.3 Preapproved Change Process

Implementation might be immediate or combined with other related changes. Organizations are normally adept at getting these changes executed within a normal operating rhythm. It is important to enforce the discipline of closing and documenting every preapproved change regardless of how simple or common it might be.

Emergency Change

An emergency change is created to restore a down system, to repair a failure, or to quickly address a risk. What each of these options represents is a current or eminent condition that has a significant impact on the business. This process must be designed to enable the implementation of the change quickly, which requires a specialized workflow for an emergency change. The approval for an emergency change can come from an ECAB (Emergency Change Approval Board) or from a senior approver who is immediately available or assigned to be on call. This can be a Change Manager, an IT director, or an IT executive. The change then moves immediately to implementation, and in many cases this occurs the same day the change request is raised. In the case of an emergency change, risk is evaluated differently.

The risk is a function of __not performing the change__ versus the approval of a normal change that considers the risk of __performing the change__.

Figure 11.4 Emergency Change Process

The very nature of an emergency change requires that the process is able to move quickly. With a system down or a service experiencing a failure, it must respond immediately to minimize the impact on the business.

This means that some compromises can be made in the interest of a quick response.

It might not be possible to convene the ECAB or to acquire the normal approval. A verbal authorization from the CIO, an IT Director, or the responsible Change Manager can be good enough to proceed. The goal is to identify a solution, perform basic testing, and implement the change on the same day. It might be necessary to identify and test more than one possible solution in order to determine the best permanent solution.

> *The world-class IT Service Management organization is very focused on the pursuit of two goals simultaneously.*

The first is to ensure the IT teams rally around an emergency change to bring the down system up, restore the failed service to normal operations, or to address a risk to the business as quickly and effectively as possible. The second is to prevent the need for an emergency change and to systematically reduce the number of these changes over time.

Recognizing that some compromises can be made in order to restore the business to normal operations, it is important to take the time to document the approval that was secured and to close and document the change, even if these steps are completed after the fact—following the implementation of the change. We need this information for a complete record, for reporting, for audit in some cases, and for trend analysis and the associated metrics.

Evaluate Change

For those normal changes that do not enter the preapproved or emergency change process, we now proceed with evaluating the change. This evaluation is a more rigorous analysis of the change and will include some form of risk assessment. This risk assessment includes a number of factors that for some organizations can be quantified as a relative score. That allows us to assign a numeric grade to the risk. These factors vary from organization to organization but can include:

✓ **Value of the Change**

✓ **Cost of Implementation**

✓ **Key Resources Required**

✓ **Probability of Success**

✓ **Impact of Failure**

✓ **Single or Multi-Organization Impact**

✓ **Urgency**

✓ **Availability of Alternative Solutions**

Figure 11.5 Risk Assessment Profile

These factors are each assessed objectively and rolled up into an overall risk report card. This is then used as a key input to what will ultimately be an approval or a rejection of the requested change. Given that most normal changes will go to the CAB, this risk profile is prepared to be ready at the assigned CAB meeting.

Another consideration at this stage, and a world-class behavior, is to consider the remediation plan. This plan is necessary in the event the change is unsuccessful and a **back-out** of the change is necessary.

> *High-performing CABs are requiring the*
> *remediation plan as a necessary part of*
> *the change request package and will not*
> *approve the change request without this*
> *fallback plan in place.*

In some cases, these plans can be reusable. With a little good planning, the remediation plan can be useful within a specific change category, and can provide a template for remediation as future change requests are submitted within the same change category.

Approve or Deny Change

The risk factors shown in Figure 11.4, along with others your organization can use to extend this list, provide more than a simple risk score. The factors should be reviewed, discussed, and debated by the CAB in order to gain an in-depth understanding of the change request. In many cases the approve/deny decision can be reached quickly and the verdict is clear. In some cases a more comprehensive analysis is necessary. The CAB is a strategic function in the business and a seat on the CAB is a key responsibility and a vote of confidence in that individual. A strong and healthy CAB is cross-functional and brings a diverse set of skills to the table.

Figure 11.6 Recommended CAB Members

This is an example roster, and your CAB membership can be adjusted and extended based on the needs of your organization. The assessment process will include the assignment of a **priority** that will be used as a point of reference as changes are managed and scheduled for implementation going forward.

In the case of a significant change, an unusually high-cost or high-risk change, or the introduction of a new service, the CAB may require a change proposal which provides a more complete and detailed description of the change, and similar to what we would expect in a business case.

> *It is a good practice to have the change initiator present the change proposal to the CAB live, and to take questions and participate in the discussion.*

In the event the CAB is unable to reach a decision (not common, but it does happen), the executive sponsor or CAB chair can cast the deciding vote, or it can be escalated to the CIO or CTO. The CAB meets on a regular schedule that will vary based on the needs of the business and the volume of change requests. Weekly meetings are a good practice.

The CAB should have a standing agenda to ensure the forum is productive and consistent. A typical structure would look like this:

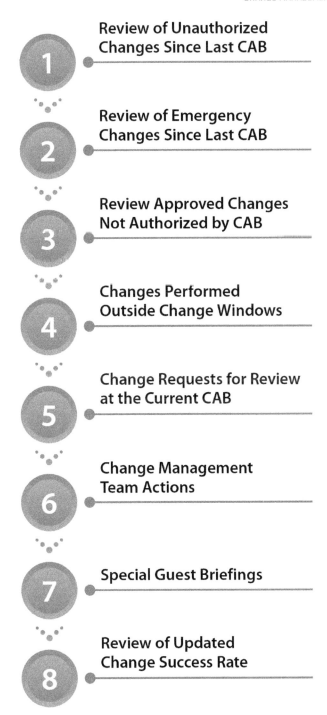

Figure 11.7 CAB Agenda

The CAB is a critical enforcement body for unauthorized changes and must look at these consistently and hold the parties accountable.

In this regard the CAB is acting as a steward of the business

and in some cases the individuals will be called to appear before the CAB and provide a detailed report on the unauthorized change. The culture of world-class IT Service Management can have no tolerance for such changes. Why? Because they represent a significant and real risk to the business as well as a source of disruption and wasted resource. Taking this a step further, when a Service Desk and IT organization are struggling and performing poorly, one of the first places we look is at the number of unauthorized changes—its negative impact is both broad and deep.

This is an important mind-set to capture and propagate. The consequences of poor Change Management are severe and can effectively cripple a business.

The CAB creates and enforces accountability for the complete change lifecycle.

This principle is an extension of the first and touches on one of the key elements of world-class IT Service Management: Accountability.

This accountability is difficult if not impossible without a strong CAB. A further extension of the CAB to consider is the addition of asset stakeholders to a virtual CAB that can be mobilized on short notice and then stood down for a period of time. This virtual CAB can make sense in the context of changes to high-profile or strategic assets that play a key role in the daily operation of the organization. These stakeholders have experience with and a deep understanding of the assets and can provide guidance and feedback to the CAB on how best to plan and execute any necessary changes.

Update IT Plans

The RFC can be denied outright, or can be returned to the initiator for revisions and resubmittal. In the case of an approval, the change moves forward to be incorporated into the broader IT plan of record. This next step is a key component of the Change Management process and protects the integrity of IT infrastructure. For example, Change Management will facilitate the addition of any approved changes to the Master Change Calendar, or Schedule of Change.

This schedule is a valuable reference for the business and provides a single, accurate view of upcoming changes, and if a change does not appear on the schedule, it should not happen. This provides a baseline of accountability and is referenced for unauthorized changes in the CAB meetings and should be on the CAB agenda (Figure 11.7).

Far beyond the CAB and the Change Management team, the Change Calendar is a useful reference for all of IT providing important visibility of upcoming maintenance, changes to existing services, retirement of services, and the introduction of new services. The Change Calendar, when put into practice, becomes a valuable cross-functional resource, and it is easy to see why.

Worth mentioning with regards to the Change Calendar is the need to establish Change Windows, during which changes should be scheduled in order to minimize disruption and negative impacts to the business. These windows are planned carefully and must be observed. These Change Windows will normally run on a weekly cycle, but this might vary depending on change volumes and the unique requirements of the organization. A typical weekly cycle would include a Change Window on Friday evening along with a second window over the weekend, Saturday morning for example, that can be used if necessary. In some cases an additional window will be slotted mid-week in the event a set of changes can't wait until the weekend or in the case of very high change volumes. Early Wednesday morning or Wednesday evening are good options for this mid-week window. Change Window durations are typically two to four hours.

> *It is a simple but vital organizational discipline to ensure changes are performed in the Change Windows.*

Changes can be combined into a logical group to form a release. The creation of a release is facilitated by Change Management along with Release Management and in coordination with all IT departments in order to maximize the synergies of changes and increase the efficiencies with which changes are introduced to the organization.

Some care must be taken to consider the Change Calendar, established Change Windows, and to avoid change collisions. The prevention of these collisions will require some additional analysis of the schedule by the Change Management and Release Management teams. These potential collisions can be avoided with a reasonable amount of planning, and this is time well spent. The cost of a collision can be high, and can result in the failure of one or more changes which can further raise the cost and broaden the negative impact to the organization.

The change implementation process should include a testing procedure. Even a lean testing process with only basic resources required reduces the risk of problems with the delivery of the change significantly. This testing should include a Remediation Plan in the event the implementation of the change fails. Remediation Plans should be repeatedly tested, improved, refined, and reused as much as possible. This is world-class behavior.

Facilitate Implementation

Change Management is a centric process, having an influence over and an interface with other Service Management processes, including Problem Management and Configuration Management. A change can be created and implemented to resolve a problem, and all changes are associated with a CI and reflected in the CMDB and by association tracked by Configuration Management. Given these relationships, the Change Management team works closely with Problem Management and Configuration Management every day and coordinates implementation of changes with these teams. Although we called on Problem and Configuration Management as example interfaces, Change Management also maintains an interface with Availability Management, Release Management, and Incident Management. Change Management will work across the organization, including these teams to facilitate the implementation of changes and to include the communications necessary to ensure the change is implemented successfully. A few necessary elements of the implementation are:

Testing Plan

Communications Plan

Remediation Plan

Post Implementation Review

Figure 11.8 Change Implementation Planning

The communication plan can be as simple as posting the Change Schedule for the week. This does not take a lot of time from the team and is far better than nothing. Consider it a baseline from which we can build a more complete plan. Change Management should also be updating the Program Management and Project Management offices frequently.

A post-implementation review is a good practice and something to be made a priority.

This review evaluates the result of the implemented change, any variances from the expected results, time and resources necessary to complete the change, any problems encountered, and recommended updates to the Test Plan in the future to help reduce the risk of recurring issues.

True, it is not convenient and yes, it takes some time, and yes, the natural focus is on the next implementation of a change, but this is another example of the discipline and accountability that creates world-class IT Service Management. Make the time and make the post-implementation review a requirement. This culture of excellence is pervasive throughout all our World-Class 12 processes and so important that we dedicate a chapter to it in Chapter 20.

This is a small reminder that Change Management done well can be a revelation in the business and a case where we can glimpse a purest ray serene.

Close and Document Change

In the case of a successful change, and following a predetermined period to validate the change is operating as expected, and following the post-implementation review, the change can be closed. Any actuals related data available on the time and resources required to implement, the hard benefits received, or other key data should be included in the record of the closed change.

There should be a defined amount of time in which the change should be closed following scheduled completion. We don't want to see changes left incomplete for an extended period of time. Change Management can work with the CAB and IT executives to determine what this timeline should be.

> *In the case of an unsuccessful change, Change Management will work with the CAB to determine the right next steps.*

This could be invoking the Remediation Plan to back out the change or it could mean modifying the change request or submitting a new request for change.

This is a case where we need to communicate well and act quickly. The remediation plan must be ready and can be implemented immediately if appropriate. In some cases this won't be necessary, and Change Management will identify the best solution for the business.

> *If ever it becomes necessary to back out a change, the post-implementation review should capture what went wrong and how the Test Plan can be improved to prevent the same problem in the future.*

We also need to evaluate if the remediation plan worked as expected, allowed a complete recovery from the failed change, and restored the service. Remediation Plans are not invoked often, so we must use this action to validate and improve the plan. When this is completed, the change can be closed.

KEY INTEGRATIONS AND PARTNERSHIPS FOR CHANGE MANAGEMENT

1. Problem Management: work closely with the Problem Managers to fully understand the relationships between changes and problems, and coordinate the change request process for these changes sponsored by the Problem Management team.
2. Configuration Management: a very important relationship exists between the configuration of IT, the service assets, and the changes that will be made to this configuration. The success of these core processes relies on the collaboration between Change and Configuration Management teams.
3. Availability Management: there exists a close but often overlooked dependency between availability and change requests. Most changes have some impact on availability, so the coordination and communication between these teams is one that requires some focus.
4. Release Management: a natural partnership exists here given the delivery of changes to the organization is facilitated through releases. Change Managers work closely with Release Management often to both plan the right release packages and to look forward and prepare for what will be delivered successfully in days and weeks to come.
5. Incident Management: a tireless linkage is active every day between incidents, problems, and changes. They must work together to achieve success and to

drive the engine of IT Service Management. A frequent, if not daily, dialogue must exist between the Incident Managers and Change Managers to both execute and plan effectively to reduce incidents and problems over time.

TIPS FOR SUCCESSFUL CHANGE MANAGEMENT

1. Change Management will have far-reaching implications and can only succeed with the necessary and appropriate cultural alignment and commitment.
2. Understand that Change Management is an evolutionary process. Success will take time and will reshape people, processes, and technology.
3. Build a strong and cross-functional CAB that has the authority to hold the business accountable to all change models and principles.
4. From the beginning, establish a goal of eliminating all unauthorized changes.
5. Every approved change must include a Back-Out Plan.
6. Establish defined Change Windows; all changes must occur in these windows.
7. Conduct a Post-Implementation Review for every successful and unsuccessful change.
8. Track the Change Success Rate and review it at every CAB meeting. World-class is 98 percent.
9. Create a document that describes your Change Management process, and keep it up to date. You will find it valuable and a popular reference.

RELEASE MANAGEMENT

Strong synergies and linkages exist between some of the processes of IT Service Management. These relationships are what enable ongoing improvements to the quality of service delivery and the reliability of IT service assets. Release Management is one process that is central to these synergies and relationships and in many ways propels the evolution of IT forward in unison with Change Management and Configuration Management. As such, we have identified Release Management as one of our Core 6 elements. It can be said that the successful implementation of Release Management is necessary to transform the traditional Help Desk or Service Desk model to true IT Service Management and to support the broader initiatives of the business related to audit, compliance, and governance.

Release Management is somewhat unique in that the implementation of this process varies more than most processes from one organization to the next. This is a reminder that exactly *how* we operationalize our IT Service Management processes is not always what is most important. It is necessary that we keep our focus on results, and in the consistent execution to the process every day and the full commitment of the organization to the same. In the case of managing releases, some organizations have found success in combining Release Management and Change Management into a single super-process. These processes are certainly closely linked, and when thoughtfully designed, this single process can work well and deliver the necessary benefits to the business. In other cases, Release Management is implemented as a full and complete process, distinct from both Change Management and Configuration Management.

These approaches can be equally effective, and

> *there is no escaping the fundamentals of good process design, good communications, naming empowered process owners, and securing the commitment of management to the initiative.*

When these fundamentals are in place, any of the twelve processes we address in the book are far more likely to be successful, even with some reasonable flaws in the details of the process model.

WHAT IT IS

Release Management provides a structured process for designing, building, testing, and delivering a successful release of changed or new CIs into production.

WHY IT IS IMPORTANT

The management of releases delivers significant value to the organization when operated and enforced appropriately:

1. Reduced risk of service interruptions
2. Faster execution of changes
3. Improved communications and fewer surprises
4. Reduced costs for change execution
5. Improved support for audit and compliance
6. More consistent operational performance
7. Ensures release plans are in place
8. Supports the design of release packages
9. Drives continuous improvements to the change success rate
10. Enhanced knowledge transfer to operational teams and business owners
11. A more consistent and ultimately proven implementation approach

HOW IT WORKS

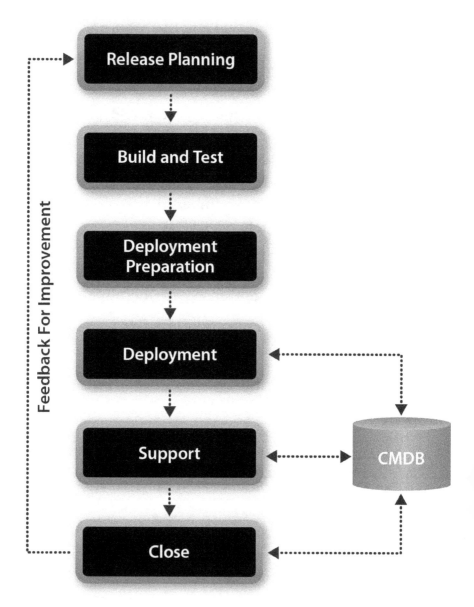

Figure 12.1 Release Management Overview

Release Planning

Release planning consists of the activities associated with the release, including the scope of the release, a working definition of the release itself, the selection of the release model to be used if appropriate, the assignment of the team that will own the release, and the primary risks associated with the release. The risks are then used as a framework to create a preliminary definition of a Test Plan, the planning of the pilot activities, a working plan for logistics, a Delivery Plan if required, and a validation of the financial and contract models if required. Finally, it is recommended that the Training Plan be considered in the early Release Planning activity.

The Training Plan is a cross-functional activity that brings teams together in a collaboration on how the organization can best prepare for the release and what skills, knowledge, and associated training will be required to help ensure a successful release. This is the most narrow context of these discussions, and beyond the immediate training needs associated with the release, there should be some discussion about longer term or general training which, although not specific to the next release, can help to better prepare the organization and individuals for future releases and overall job performance.

What the Release Planning activity does is create the opportunity for this important dialogue that might not otherwise happen.

Build and Test

This element captures the detailed execution of the build and test of the release. Build and test must go hand in hand because one element is not viable without the other. Build activities include assembling the individual components being managed by the change process that will together make up the release. Depending on the business model and the type of organization, this could be a single component or a larger number. The assembly of the right related components are referred to as a package. The release must be tested in a manner that demonstrates the release will meet the goals and objectives of the release and in a manner that addresses the risks identified in Release Planning and

> *in an environment representative of production, but not in production itself.*

This is the value of the pilot, to demonstrate a rigorous test that closely models the ultimate production environment. The pilot can also validate training and documentation have been properly delivered or that more attention is required. Service testing can add value by verifying the components of the release work as expected when together. This can also be referred to as Service Integration Testing.

> *This is all about testing how elements work together, or inter-operate, versus the performance of the individual items.*

The activity might require additional attention if the interoperability of the release components is considered to be a significant risk. The Service Test can also evaluate the portability of the release from pilot to the production environment. This is often a final step in the Service Testing process and should be managed as a full readiness test process. It is very important that rigor and careful execution are used in final Readiness Testing.

Deployment Preparation

In the first stage of the process, Release Planning, preliminary deployment preparation occurs, and now we execute a more detailed sweep of the necessary preparations for deployment. This includes a final readiness check for the delivery of the release package, a comprehensive and updated assessment of the risks associated with the release, a risk mitigation plan for each critical risk (it is simply not practical to create a risk mitigation plan for every risk), an evaluation of any changes to the key business requirements since the initial Release Planning occurred, as it may have been weeks or even months since these activities occurred, and validation that the necessary training has been completed and the release communication plan and timeline are in place and ready to launch. At this stage of deployment preparation, it is important to differentiate between five primary types of deployments:

1. The upgrade or modification of an existing service
2. The release of an all-new service
3. The retirement of a service
4. The merger or consolidation of two or more services

5. The transfer of a service from one organization to another

There are of course other types of deployments, but these five address the high majority of what is typical for a release. While these deployment types share a common set of elements, the specific type will necessitate some unique considerations. For example, the release of an all-new service would normally drive a more extensive training and communication plan versus the upgrade of an existing service. In the case of the transfer of a service, particular attention must be given to knowledge transfer and the financial and administrative considerations associated with the transition of the service.

Deployment

At the initiation of deployment, the plans finalized in the work of deployment preparation launch into action. At this critical stage of Release Management, it is vital to constantly evaluate the risks identified in the deployment preparation stage. Think of this as an early warning mechanism. Once deployment has begun, the early identification of a failure or lapse in execution can mean the difference between success and failure for the overall deployment. It is important to catch the issues early in the deployment and take the necessary actions. Key activities in deployment include:

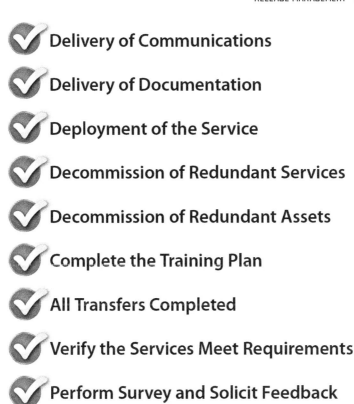

✔ Delivery of Communications

✔ Delivery of Documentation

✔ Deployment of the Service

✔ Decommission of Redundant Services

✔ Decommission of Redundant Assets

✔ Complete the Training Plan

✔ All Transfers Completed

✔ Verify the Services Meet Requirements

✔ Perform Survey and Solicit Feedback on the Deployment

Figure 12.2 Deployment Highlights

These activities will continue well beyond the go-live date of the deployment, and the release team must remain diligent during this time before declaring the release a success. For example, the verify and feedback activities can require several weeks to complete depending on the size of the organization and the number of users.

Support

With the completion of deployment, support of the release must be ready and initiated immediately. In some cases, which include a release that carries high risks, some elements of support will begin before the deployment ends. Organizations should expect and plan for a higher level of activity immediately following the deployment. This post-deployment period is critical to ensuring a successful deployment. A few key activities for this period include:

1. The SLAs associated with the new service are finalized and accepted.
2. Users of the service are experiencing normal operations.
3. Communications and training have been completed.
4. Any initial issues have been reported, logged, and resolved.
5. The deployment debrief with all process owners and business stakeholders has been completed.
6. Performance metrics are achieved for a defined post-deployment period. This is typically fifteen to thirty days.

When these six elements have been achieved to the satisfaction of the business, the transition is made to standard, ongoing support of the new service. The determination of what is "satisfactory" can be made with Release Managers, Change Managers, and Service Level Managers reviewing all available data and evaluating the execution of the complete release.

Review and Close

The majority of Close activities should be standard for every release. This creates consistency and discipline of performance from release to release. In addition to the core set of Close activities, special activities may augment the standard rule due to unique considerations of a specific release. In order to close the deployment, the following items should be completed:

Document Recommended Improvements for the Next Deployment

Conduct a Review With the Release Team and the Business Shareholders

Conduct Audit to Verify Completion of All Activities and That All Records Have Been Updated

Established Metrics and SLA's Document All Known Errors and Workaround as a Deliverable to Ongoing Operations

Complete Final Checklist for the Transition of the Service to Production

Figure 12.3 Key Deployment Close Activities

There is an important opportunity here that should not be lost related to incremental and continuous improvement. This is a consistent theme throughout practical Service Management and is essentially a *lifestyle*. Note that a majority of the Close activities are related to improvements, report cards, metrics, and reviews, and this is collectively the information we need to get better.

The importance of this process can't be
overstated.

KEY PARTNERSHIPS AND INTEGRATIONS FOR RELEASE MANAGEMENT

1. Change Management: a natural partnership that must be in lockstep with Release Management on the strategy, scope, and execution of all changes and releases.
2. Asset and Configuration Management: the fundamental objective of Release is to deliver new or changed CIs to the organization, which creates a clear and unbreakable linkage to the processes that describe and manage the CIs themselves.
3. Problem Management: the actions associated with Problem Management often rely on changes and releases, and with this comes a high level of communication and coordination to ensure problems are closed as quickly as possible through this cross-functional work.
4. Service Level Management: Service Levels are a function of successful releases, both good and bad. These teams work closely together to maximize the leverage of releases to the benefit of service levels.

TIPS FOR SUCCESSFUL RELEASE MANAGEMENT

1. Invest in a good communication plan. This avoids surprises and helps all of the organization to be prepared.
2. Build a test plan and pilot phase that closely mirrors the production environment. Not easy, but vital.

3. Don't overlook Service Testing. This ensures every-thing works together as expected.

4. Assign an individual to own the risk assessment and mitigation plan. This plan must take a critical look at all elements of the release, and we need a strong owner driving this.

5. Double-check the early warning mechanisms. An effective early warning of a potential failure can spare the organization significant resources and time. There also exists the risk of an unhappy and unproductive customer in the event of a failed release.

6. Ensure the SLAs for the new service are finalized and well understood.

7. Take the time to complete the release scorecard and recommendations for future improvements.

AVAILABILITY MANAGEMENT

Availability Management is a vastly underrated process. Its value is fundamental: to ensure the availability of services and the supporting infrastructure is prepared to meet or exceed what the business requires. Failing to meet these needs can have an immediate and significant impact on customer satisfaction, customer loyalty, and ultimately revenue. It is critical that we get this right, while recognizing the needs of the organization will continue to evolve and the pull of change will not be denied.

WHAT IT IS

Availability Management will lead the planning, design, implementation, and oversight of the availability of IT services and the infrastructure components that make these services possible. This process combines a view of today with what will be required in the future, including consideration of the Service Portfolios pipeline.

WHY IT IS IMPORTANT

The success of any service is only possible with the necessary level of availability. When all is working as designed, availability allows the business to be at its best, and the level and quality of service are maximized. High availability is simply assumed. However, the moment availability suffers, everybody notices and everything changes. The loss of a critical service will shift the organization to crisis management, and the impact can be serious. This must be avoided, which brings us back to Availability Management. Key benefits include:

1. Delivering availability performance that meets or exceeds known requirements
2. Assisting in the rapid resolution of any availability-related issues
3. Partnering with the business to create a long-term availability and investment plan
4. Working closely with Change and Release Management to evaluate and mitigate the risks to availability of planned changes
5. Strategically evaluating the improvement of customer satisfaction through availability
6. Proactive monitoring and measurement of service performance and availability

HOW IT WORKS

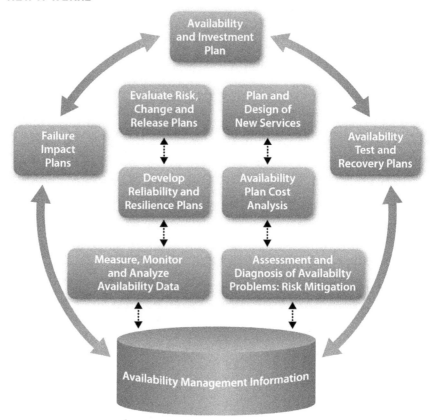

Figure 13.1 Availability Management At Work

The construction of a strong Availability Management process requires a diverse mix of planning and execution activities. These activities must include both proactive and reactive tasks and will include rigorous analysis of data in combination with long-term planning based on strategic direction and evolving tactics.

All activities leverage an extensive availability information database which reflects the unique needs of this process with regards to data analysis, scenario development, risk evaluation, cost modeling, and services planning. Figure 13.1 shows an overview of the Availability Management process, and we will explore each of the eight components in turn.

Measure, Monitor, and Analyze Availability Data

Effective Availability Management requires a commitment to data analysis and monitoring activities. This is different than some other processes that follow more of a defined sequence of actions and decision gates. The goal of Availability Management is to ensure the availability of services at a level that meets or exceeds requirements. This simply can't be done without careful analysis of all known availability data.

An important consideration in the data analysis activity is recognizing different contexts for the data. This would include the technology along with user and business views, and each is very different. Expanding this scope a bit further, there is another dimension to the data that must be considered: It is not a matter of availability alone being a single dimension to the information we have. There are at least four important dimensions, each related but each unique:

Figure 13.2 Key Factors for Availability

We don't want to make this too complicated, but it's necessary to recognize that we must approach this process on
three distinct but related and sometimes intersecting planes.

Figure 13.3 The Dimensions of Availability

The glue that brings all this together are the services. In the enormous ocean of data and the ensuing analysis, it helps to remember this is all about ensuring the service is ready when our users and the business need it.

Assessment and Diagnosis of Failures

We can learn a lot from a failure to meet the availability requirement of a service. Each failure will be analyzed by Availability Management to determine the events leading up to a failure, the failure itself, and the timeline to restore service following the failure.

In the event of a failure, effective communications and a prompt response can lead to no loss of customer satisfaction and, in some cases, an increase.

> *People understand that failures will occur, and the events and the speed of activity following a failure say a lot about the quality of an organization.*

To fully understand a failure, the recovery process, and the restoration of the service, it is important to consider each event in the timeline and a measurement of each time segment.

Figure 13.4 Incident to Restored Service Timeline

Figure 13.4 shows an overview of this important timeline. While it is important to measure each of the four elapsed time segments, the key is the elapsed time to restore normal service. There is a standard IT metric, mean time to restore service (MTRS), associated with this response speed, and a goal should be defined for each service.

Broadening this view, we also need to look at the time between failures, another key metric. The mean time between failures (MTBF) provides a different set of factors to be considered. Frequent failures, even with a fast elapsed time to restore service, is a pattern that creates serious challenges for the organization. The analysis of a failure is not complete without another, more micro-level assessment. We need to look at each of the three elapsed time segments that precede restoration of service: the time to detect, time to diagnose, and time to repair.

> *It is necessary to understand each of these timelines within the timeline in order to create a risk mitigation plan for the future.*

For example, if we are seeing delays in the detection of the failure, we can't improve the time to restore service without first addressing the elapsed time to detect.

This begins to get at the topic of self-healing incidents that we will address in the final chapter on the future of IT Service Management.

Develop Reliability and Resiliency Plans

Although related terms and often part of the same discussion, reliability and resiliency are different, and both play an important role in managing availability of a service. Reliability measures how long a service or a component can perform as expected without a failure. Higher reliability indicates longer periods without failure, and lower reliability indicates shorter periods without failure.

Resilience is an important and sometimes overlooked performance characteristic. Resilience is the ability of a component or a service to combat failure or, in the event of a failure, to recover quickly and fully. Resilience plays a vital role because it can offset the risk of reliability that is less than ideal. For example, if we have a service that is currently performing at a lower level of reliability, a high resilience rating would allow the service to recover quickly in the event of a failure. This quick recovery then minimizes the impact to users and customers.

Similarly, if our resilience is currently at a lower than desired level, a high level of reliability can offset the risk associated with a lower resilience rating. In IT Service Management we love our metrics, and in some cases we can overdo it, diluting our focus on metrics that are truly critical—some of which we mentioned earlier. One such metric is the mean time between failures (MTBF). This is measurement of the reliability of a service.

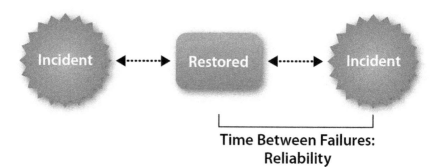

Time Between Failures: Reliability

Figure 13.5 The Reliability of a Service

For each service, we should have a goal defined for the MTBF. This target is set by Availability Management, and in coordination with the Service Portfolio Manager, this target is defined for all new services.

To clarify the measure of resilience, and to expand on the timeline we showed in Figure 13.4, we will zoom in on the mean time to restore service (MTRS).

Time to Restore Service: Resilience

Figure 13.6 The Resilience of a Service

While excellent resilience can help offset weaker reliability and strong reliability can offset lower resilience, the world-class model is strong reliability complemented by strong resilience. We should consistently measure and communicate both the MTBF and MTRS metrics.

Availability Plan Cost Analysis

The goal of availability for each service must be supported by a plan that details how the organization will perform at the necessary level. In building this plan, the primary focus should be on what is required to hit the availability target. This plan should include a number of elements:

1. Required service assets
2. Available support personnel and skill sets
3. Required components
4. Target MTBF
5. Target MTRS
6. Redundancy plan
7. Key procedures and policies
8. Maintenance plan

We will explore the Availability Plan later, but it is important to note here that after creating a draft of the Availability Plan, we must then calculate the cost of delivering the availability proposed in this plan.

We simply can't ignore cost, and this must be balanced with the performance levels described in the plan.

This process of striking the right balance between availability and cost might require a few iterations to get it right. It can be helpful to develop a few availability scenarios and the associated cost of each. This allows the organization to understand and to quantify what improvements are possible with an additional level of investment. The scenarios take what might normally be abstract and make it more real and more measurable. The different scenarios, normally three or four, ranging from entry level availability to a high level at or very near 100 percent, can then be debated and reviewed with management before selecting the best overall and affordable plan.

Develop Failure Impact Plans

As we walk through a more complete view of Availability Management, we begin to appreciate the multiple dimensions of delivering and managing availability. And of course we must do this at a very high level in order to operate a model that we can consider to be world-class and earn the trust of the business every day.

In the previous section we looked at the balance between cost and availability as viewed through the lens of reliability and resilience. Now, we expand that discussion further to consider the impact of failure. Just as it is not possible to determine the best plan for availability without considering cost, we can't truly appreciate the merits and risks of any availability scenario without including an assessment of failure impact.

As with our reliability and resilience plans, it can help to develop discrete failure scenarios, with each considering:

1. Assumptions for the failure, including duration and scope
2. The capital cost of the failure
3. Impact to the satisfaction of users and customers
4. Lost revenue, if any
5. Potential loss of renewals
6. Impact to employee productivity
7. Impact to service SLAs
8. Summary of other impacts

With these failure impact scenarios, we can then triangulate the level of potential availability, with the cost to deliver service at that level, with the impact of failure as we increment or decrement availability.

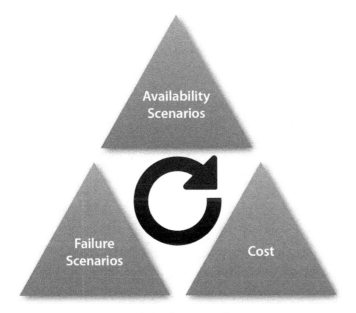

Figure 13.7 Availability and Cost Scenarios

This is an important debate for the business, and as is normally the case, we are able to make the best decision when armed with the best information. We also need to consider the current state of the organization. For example, if the business is in a strong financial position but user/customer satisfaction is lower than our target level, we might choose to make a larger capital investment to increase availability. This reminds us of the strategic connection between Availability Management, Service Portfolios, and running the business.

Evaluate Risk in Change and Release Plans

Changes and releases can improve availability, but they also represent risk as they can be making changes to the components that enable the availability of a service. Availability Management should work closely with Change Management and Release Management as a collaborator in first evaluating and then mitigating any risks to availability.

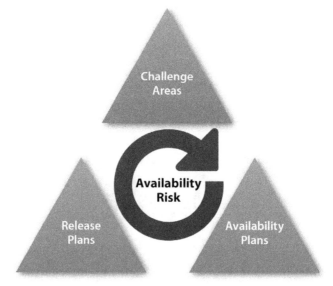

Figure 13.8 A Broader Evaluation of Risk

This represents another important triangulation in the business. We must make changes; this is a given. But Change Managers must consider many factors and can't be overly focused on the implications to availability. Availability Management can provide an important part of the checks and balances that make up world-class IT Service Management by proactively filling this role and by working with both Change Managers and Release Managers to review these plans, to provide an availability assessment, and finally to develop recommendations to reduce any risks.

This connection to Change Management and Release Management is not a traditional partnership, so Availability Management should be proactive in forming this relationship.

> *We covered the need to assess risk in change and release plans, and a productive method to employ in the pursuit of reduced risk is a redundancy plan.*

Redundancy is a method employed to improve the availability and reliability of services and components. This redundancy will have a cost associated with it, so it must be considered in the cost/availability review and planning process.

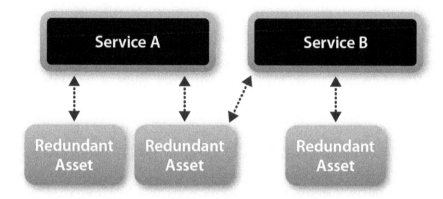

Figure 13.9 Service Redundancy Model

Redundancy is a very effective strategy and has been proven for over a century in military, industrial, and mechanical applications. As the profile of mission-critical systems delivered by IT grows in the business, we can leverage this valuable model where the cost/availability tradeoff makes sense.

Figure 13.9 shows a simple example where redundant assets support Service A and Service B, and a single asset is shared between the two services. In the event of a failure of the primary assets that support the service, the redundant assets are activated to keep the service running.

A *Hot Standby* model will allow an instantaneous activation of the redundant asset, and a *Cold Standby* model will require some time to activate the asset. This time varies depending on the service, the complexity of the asset, and the process required for activation. Note the Hot Standby model has some advantages but is also significantly more expensive to operate in most cases.

Plan and Design of New Services

The planning of new services is part of a core set of strategic activities in IT Service Management. This activity is addressed in more detail in the chapter on Service Portfolios (Chapter 15), and it is a testament to Availability Management that service availability must be a member of the team enabling the planning process.

Another partner in this process is Financial Management, with cost and benefits being a consistent theme running through many of our processes. I like the concept of checks and balances as a model to capture the accountability and teamwork at the core of world-class IT Service Management. Another example of these connections is present here in this section on the planning of new services in the context of Availability Management.

Figure 13.10 New Services Planning Model

To emphasize the point made earlier, no new service can be introduced successfully without an Availability Plan that creates a satisfied user day in and day out. This level of consistency has been made throughout the book, and I have used the terms *every day*, *day after day*, and *day in and day out* because this captures a strategy, a mind-set, and a commitment that is at the core of world-class IT Service Management. The essence of this mind-set is that what we do must be done extremely well, but it must also be trustworthy and consistent. A big part of the excellence associated with world-class is the delivery of services which are in turn built on models that support fast, consistent, and reliable decision making and service. You get the idea.

To this end, Figure 13.10 represents a further expansion of the

dynamic teamwork and accountability model that creates a level of healthy debate and brings our best ideas together

to ultimately create the best possible result: in this case, a plan for a new service that includes world-class availability. It is far more effective to design in the necessary level of availability from the very beginning of the design process for a new service.

Availability Test and Recovery Plans

As we have so much at stake with the availability of services, testing and recovery plans must be part of every new service rollout and a key activity in the daily work of Availability Management. A few things to be considered in the Availability Test Plan:

✓ Testing of Most Common Failure Cases

✓ Simulate Recovery From Failure Cases

✓ Testing of High Risk Failure Cases

✓ Conduct Training for Recovery Process

✓ Identification of High Risk Components

✓ Test Plan to Verify Targeted MTBF

✓ Publish Availability Test Schedule

✓ Simulations to Verify Targeted MTRS Including the Recovery Process

✓ Conduct Training for Repair Process

✓ Publish Preventive Maintenance Schedule

Figure 13.11 Key Issues for Availability Test Plan

Proactive and aggressive testing can reduce risk and improve availability performance over time. The test activities shown in Figure 13.11 should not be limited to standard test cases.

Testing activity should include test cases that accurately reproduce actual conditions from past service or component failures.

These activities should be conducted on a test system that mirrors the production system to the greatest extent possible. The Test Plan should also include high-risk test cases that represent new threats, changes in the environment, or the testing of new services that have not yet failed and have no history to draw from.

We can utilize automated testing and simulation tools. These tools have improved greatly in the past ten years and can reduce the risk of failure by:

1. Generating a high volume of test cases
2. Ad-hoc testing to identify new risks
3. Tracking and logging of test failures
4. Simulations to support testing and recovery

This all begins with a commitment to the testing process and extending this activity into recovery planning. History will give us a good indication of risk, and we must take full advantage of the failures of the past in preparing us for the future. We can then add to the mix the use of testing tools to help identify vulnerabilities that are not known today.

Availability and Investment Plan

Creating the right Availability Plan for all services and for the business is very much about investment. A good plan does not come for free and does not happen by accident. It is the product of thoughtful and strategic investment, and as such I have these elements sharing the title of this section.

It can help to remember what our goals are for this plan and the process:

1. Availability of the IT assets that enable the delivery of services
2. Meeting or exceeding the needs of the business as it relates to acccss to services
3. Ensuring the availability of services required to serve employees and customers
4. To leverage the plan as a platform to drive cooperation between Incident Management, Problem Management, Change Management, Service Portfolios, and Financial Management
5. To demonstrate and quantify the value of the plan in order to overcome the risks of inadequate commitment from the business and inadequate funding

If we are able to meet these five goals and others that become apparent in the pursuit of these five, then we have succeeded in delivering great value to the business and accelerated our progress in the journey to world-class IT Service Management.

KEY PARTNERSHIPS AND INTEGRATIONS FOR AVAILABILITY MANAGEMENT

1. Incident Management: this team provides a good source of historical incident information as an input

to the Availability Test Plan that in turn can better ensure a higher level of future availability performance. This partnership extends further to include current and recent service failure analysis as a key input to the Availability Plan.

2. Problem Management: another partner in the process of creating more complete and comprehensive Test Plans and in defining an Availability Plan that moves to a proactive approach for reducing Problem volumes over time. As with Incident Management, this alliance looks at service failures to determine how the Availability Plan can be further enhanced.

3. Change Management: in recognizing there is a close linkage between changes and availability performance, partnership and coordination are important to ensure that the teams are working in unison to meet the dual goals of successful Changes and high availability.

4. Service Portfolios: the right level of availability is fundamental to the Service Portfolio process, and Availability Management will partner with the Service Portfolio Managers throughout the lifecycle of every service. High availability will likely result in a successful introduction of a new service, and, conversely, poor availability will likely bring failure.

5. Financial Management: cost, investment, and availability have strong dependencies, and a high level of coordination is required between the Financial Management and Availability Management teams in order to strike the right balance of investment and availability performance.

TIPS FOR SUCCESSFUL AVAILABILITY MANAGEMENT

1. From the beginning, establish a working relationship with the Incident, Problem, Change, Service Portfolios, and Financial Management teams.
2. Make availability a mandatory element of the planning for new services.
3. The assessment of failures is as important as the development of the Availability Plan and will make the plan better.
4. Measure and communicate both MTBF and MTRS indicators of availability performance. Emphasize the importance of speed of recovery as a means to reduce the impact of a failure.
5. Leverage redundancy as a strategy to significantly enhance availability.
6. Work with the business to balance cost with the required level of availability. This is a strategic business decision and should receive high visibility with management.
7. Proactive testing goes hand in hand with the Availability Plan and is not an afterthought. Make testing of service availability a business competency.

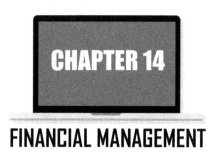

FINANCIAL MANAGEMENT

Although not our most complex process, Financial Management is an important one. Financial Management is not often in scope for the early phases of an IT Service Management implementation, but it holds the key for creating cost, benefits, and risk awareness across the organization where this awareness often did not exist before. This is also where cost accountability for existing and new services begins, and it creates a framework for a business case approach to future service-related investments.

WHAT IT IS

Financial Management provides essential financial data to the organization in order to support the budgeting and business case process and ultimately to help ensure the successful and cost-effective delivery of services. A further benefit is creating a dialogue of cost awareness and financial accountability that will reshape the thought process and dialogue around service investments. This will have a strong cultural influence over time and shape the thinking of all those teams responsible for delivering services to the organization.

WHY IT IS IMPORTANT

Financial Management creates a new level of cost awareness in the IT organization as well as across the business, and with this awareness comes a number of important benefits, including:

1. Improved control of IT operations
2. Ability to create business cases for IT services
3. Accelerated decision-making
4. Improved service management budgets
5. Creates new financial controls and metrics
6. Complements Service Catalog and chargebacks
7. Supports the definition of service value
8. Enhances Service Portfolio management and the related investment analysis
9. Creates a cultural shift, including a new level of awareness around costs and benefits for all that we do in IT
10. Having a fiscal management process in place will naturally lead to cost avoidance benefits in the future, often related to the upgrade of existing systems and technologies that no longer meet the needs of the business.
11. Connects the accountability of the front-line teams to mid-level management and to senior management. These linkages are critical to the broader

financial awareness necessary for great IT Service Management exccution.

HOW IT WORKS

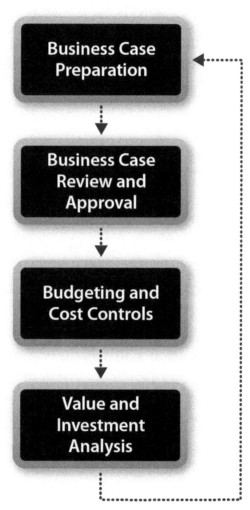

Figure 14.1 Financial Management Overview

Business Case Preparation

A business case is a short document that provides an overview of a potential new investment. For the sake of this discussion, we will assume this relates to a new service. In the most general sense, a business case can and should be used for any new project or investment in virtually any business. I have shown the business case as the first activity because it is a good catalyst for Financial Management, and it drives a number of important activities and related thoughts. The creation of the business case, and the understanding necessary to win approval for a new investment, changes the culture of an organization. It creates more accountability and encourages more disciplined and structured decision-making.

The business case should consist of at least five primary elements:

1. Overview
2. Costs
3. Benefits
4. Risks
5. Recommendation

The **Overview** should be considered an Executive Summary and provide a clear and succinct description of the investment under consideration. This is a good opportunity to provide some context and key facts that should be considered.

The **Costs** summary should provide a complete and quantified list of all direct and indirect costs. It is important

that some time is taken to make this summary both complete and accurate. Without this diligence, decisions can be
made—and often very large investments—that can have a
significant impact on the business, based on incomplete or
inaccurate cost information. It should be expected that the
actual costs captured in the investment analysis phase that
comes later should be within a reasonable margin of error
as a variance from the cost summary in the business case. A
good target for this variance is ten to fifteen percent.

The **Benefits** summary describes the positive impact to the
business. This can include both financial benefits and other non-financial value. For example, time savings, reduced
cycle times, and improved satisfaction levels are desirable
benefits. In some cases there will be more immediate tactical benefits and longer-term strategic benefits, and it is a
good practice to capture both. As with the costs, take the
time to provide as accurate a quantification of these benefits as possible.

As with any new service and investment, there will be inherent **Risks** that must be described in the business case. A
complete description of these risks and a preliminary mitigation plan for each are critical to creating a balanced and
insightful business case. Accuracy here is paramount, and
the investment analysis phase should include a review of
past business cases and the risks described in each. Were
the risks accurate? Did issues arise during the implementation of a new service that were not captured as a risk in the
business case? Is there a pattern of issues across multiple
new investments and new services that should be reflected
in future business cases? While writing the business case,

maintain a mind-set that risks are as important as the cost summary and benefits summary. This reinforces the checks and balances and accountability that are so important for world-class IT Service Management.

The final section in the business case is the **Recommendation**. With careful consideration given to the costs, benefits, and risks, this is the net course of action supported and recommended by the business case team. A typical model would see the business case prepared by the business owners who would have operational responsibility for the new service, and the business case brought to a financial/IT budget committee that includes the CIO, CTO, CFO, VP IT, VP Services, and other similar management and executive roles. The review of the recommendation should include lots of discussion and debate. Ultimately the only necessary result is a good decision for the business. The business case makes this improved decision-making possible.

Business Case Review and Approval

Business case preparation is an investment of time and resource that pays back to the organization in many ways. This becomes apparent in the review of business case(s). A well-prepared business case will not necessarily be approved, but it allows the process to be far more productive and helps to ensure a better decision.

Good information creates a path to a good decision.

One or more business cases are reviewed when the business/budget committee meets. This group typically consists of three to five members, including management and executive leadership. The frequency of meetings varies, with the most common schedule being monthly or quarterly. The senior member, often the CIO or CFO, will serve as chair and facilitate the review process and the final decision. The committee will have a budget to work within, and any approved business case must fit into the Cap Ex and Op Ex budgets and comply with the budgetary and controls guidelines of the current fiscal year. The committee will review multiple business cases during a meeting; this both makes the best use of time and allows business cases to be compared and contrasted with other business cases under consideration and likely competing for the same budget and resource.

The reality of today's IT Service Management organization is that budgets will be tight, but the organization is under pressure to deliver high-quality services in a manner that is faster and more efficient. And

increasingly, faster is the key element, taking priority over efficient.

In this paradigm, efficient is nice, but fast is paramount. The real meaning of *efficient* is the subject of much discussion, but normally derives from delivering a measurable and satisfactory result in a way that results in a quantifiable savings of time, resources, or money. This is a fundamental principle that is important to world-class IT Service Management and one I learned a deep appreciation for while working at the Johnson Space Center in Houston, Texas, during the 1980s. More on this later.

The business cases delivering the most compelling benefits at an acceptable cost are the most likely to be approved. Some level of "competition" between business cases is a good thing and quite practical. After all, these proposals are competing for the same budget, resource, and organizational bandwidth.

After careful review, discussion, and debate, each business case will be approved, denied, or returned with a request for clarifications or more information.

Location	Item	Cost
San Jose, CA	Wireless Access Point	$4,000
Phoenix, AZ	Controller and Wireless Access Point	$13,500
Dublin, Ireland	Wireless Access Point and Controller	$12,000
Frankfurt, Germany	Wireless Access Point	$5,800
TOTAL		$35,300

Figure 14.2 Global Wi-Fi Upgrade Costs Summary

Area	Improvement
Access Speed	2x
Improved Range	20%
Employee Productivity	2-5%
Ease of Expansion	+100 Employees

Figure 14.3 Global Wi-Fi Upgrade Benefits Summary

Budgeting and Cost Controls

With an approved business case, the requesting individual/ team mobilizes for the implementation of the investment. The approved budget will be issued by the budget committee along with a framework of cost controls to regulate progress going forward. This is an important transition, as even a simple budget target and a cost control process will create the visibility and accountability critical to successful Financial Management.

With the budget agreed to and released for spending,

we want to establish a cadence for cost controls that will include updates on actual spending against the budget.

A good schedule is weekly, normally on a Monday or a Friday. Spending numbers are released that show any spending variance against the budget. This can also be done every two weeks but no less often. Frequent updates lead to fewer surprises and allow adjustments to be made if actual spending begins to deviate from the plan. The budget committee should also have visibility into the cost control process to track the project and be ready to review exceptions if needed. Normally this is run as a project, and standard project management applies.

Value and Investment Analysis

To close the full Financial Management lifecycle, a value and investment analysis must be conducted following the completion of the project. In order to get a clear and complete view of value and benefits, it is necessary for some time to pass prior to the review. A typical interval of elapsed time would be about six months, but more time could be needed. The target date should be agreed to when the business case is approved and then updated when the project is completed. What we are looking for in the analysis is:

1. Quantified value received
2. How does the real value and benefit compare to what was projected in the business case?
3. How did the final real investment compare to the projected costs in the business case?
4. Review of any setbacks in the project and how to prevent these from occurring in the future
5. Address any actions or questions from the budget committee

While it is important to keep the discipline of this analysis alive, the report and process should be simple and lean.

KEY INTEGRATIONS AND PARTNERSHIPS FOR FINANCIAL MANAGEMENT

1. Service Portfolios: this represents a close collaboration with Financial Management as the launch of all new services, the retirement of existing services, and the investment in an active service should all be done within the context of a business case and a full understanding of the elements contained therein.

2. Service Catalog: as a growing and dynamic vehicle for the offering of services, Service Catalog creates the opportunity to introduce cost awareness and ultimately cost accountability across the organization. Whether it be an immediate implementation or a phased implementation over time, Financial Management will partner with the Service Catalog team to develop the right cost strategy.

3. Finance and Administration: a natural partnership exists here, often lying dormant but ready to be awakened, between the corporate finance and admin function and the Financial Management process within IT. Together these teams can both plan and execute the Financial Management process and the business case structure—for example, for IT—and then collaborate and share as the process is operating over time.

4. Change Management: many changes represent a meaningful investment in some form and should be evaluated with a view to the financial considerations

inherent to this element. For major changes it can make sense to require a business case to fully understand the costs, risks, and benefits as part of the Change Review and Approval process.

5. IT Leadership: the introduction of a Financial Management process into IT will normally include sponsorship by IT leadership, including the CIO, as there are many implications to the launch and success of this process. This is a great example of the cultural shift we refer to throughout the book and represents a seed of change; when financial accountability is introduced to IT, the impact will be dramatic.

TIPS FOR SUCCESSFUL FINANCIAL MANAGEMENT

1. Be mindful to keep this process focused on the key elements and avoid unnecessary overhead.

2. Business cases should be thoughtful and insightful. Don't let this become an exercise to fill in a template.

3. The business case review process should be tough and demanding. We are competing for precious company resources, and only the very best plans are approved.

4. The Cost Control and Reporting process must be well defined and understood before the project starts. This should not be addressed after the project is underway, as this could result in delays.

5. The accountability of the value and investment analysis is vital and must never be skipped or compromised. Successful Financial Management is not possible without it.

CHAPTER 15

SERVICE PORTFOLIOS

The inclusion of Service Portfolios in our World-Class 12 might raise a few eyebrows, so let me explain. All IT Service Management processes are important and have been proven over time. Most are tactical models and used to operate IT every day and to deliver necessary services. This is as it should be. Incident Management is one good example. It is simply not possible to run the Service Desk without some form of Incident Management. But Incident Management is very much optimized around an incident and in restoring normal service as quickly as possible in a tactical manner.

Service Portfolios is one of a few strategic processes that look more broadly at the business and evaluate the future needs of the organization as a whole. What services will be required, what shape will they take, when should they be offered, and how best can they be delivered? This is a very simplistic summary and just the beginning of the process.

So, while many IT Service Management organizations have not implemented a Service Portfolio process today, I expect this to change in the next five years.

A growing number of companies are maturing and becoming great at the Core 6 processes. This then enables companies to look at the next steps in realizing the vision of world-class service delivery. We should expect Service Portfolios to enjoy more attention and to bring a more strategic view and mind-set to the business.

As such, we will review the fundamentals of this process to help you get started when the time comes.

WHAT IT IS

The Service Portfolio is a complete set of services offered to meet the needs of each customer, both internal and external, served by the service provider. The management of Service Portfolios must include all the resources necessary to provide each service and the assessment of value delivered.

WHY IT'S IMPORTANT

Service Portfolios provide an essential link between the Service Management organization and the customer. Key elements of Service Portfolios include:

1. Understanding the services needed by customers
2. Defining the set of services to be offered

3. Measuring the cost of delivering each
4. Capturing the value of the service
5. Quantifying the demand
6. Identifying the resources required
7. Gaining a holistic understanding of the evolution of services to be delivered in the future and the strategy driving this evolution

HOW IT WORKS

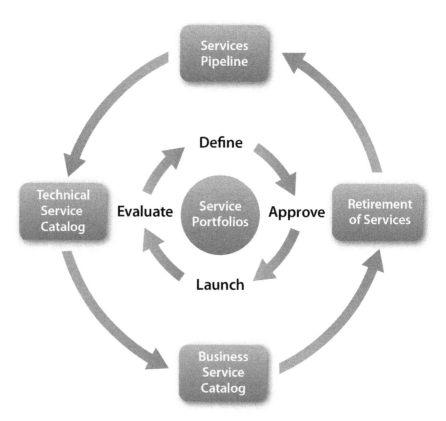

Figure 15.1 The Service Portfolio Process

Services Pipeline

The Services Pipeline provides a short-term and a long-term view of services offered to the business. This must be a complete view and will include all the related tools and technologies necessary to launch and operate the service. This provides a more holistic understanding of the costs, risks, resource requirements, and benefits associated with the service. There is a vital discussion and analysis that must occur as each service moves through the service life-cycle. Think of this as spanning the time from initial concept to service retirement.

The business case process discussed in Chapter 17 (Financial Management) is a necessary part of the services pipeline activity in order to fully vet each potential service vying for company resources. Another important related discussion is that of Availability Management and the level of availability required for the service. This can have many implications. A few things to keep in mind for the services pipeline:

1. Develop an intermediate term, six months to two years, and a longer term, two- to five -year services roadmap.
2. New services affect most of the organization, so the Portfolio Manager must be a liaison across the business.
3. The process can also provide a three- to six -month launch schedule for new services that are approved and budgeted.

Technical Service Catalog

The Services Portfolio will include both internal-facing services, business services, and customer-facing services. Some forward-looking companies are now taking advantage of the convenience and efficiency of the service catalog by offering a Technical Service Catalog that represents technologies, applications, and projects. Each of these entities will be managed through a lifecycle, and the visibility, updates, current status, and more can be managed through the Technical Service Catalog. This experience would not normally be offered directly to customers, but there is a direct and synergistic relationship between these technical offerings and what is offered to the field teams, support, sales, marketing teams, and customers.

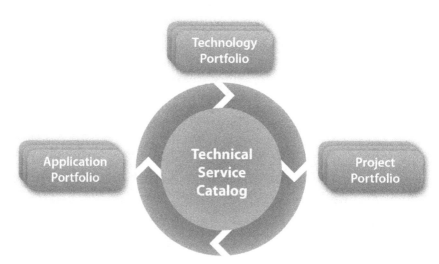

Figure 15.2 The Technical Service Catalog

The orientation of the Technical Service Catalog is more focused on the visibility and communication of status, schedule, and current attributes of the objects in the catalog versus the more business and transaction orientation of the Business Service Catalog. However, the navigation, look, and experience will be very similar. We take a closer look at these qualities in Chapter 9 on Service Catalog.

Business Service Catalog

The Business Service Catalog will offer a number of diverse services with an orientation aligned with the business. These service requests can provide a set of cross-functional services, focused single organization services, customer-facing services, and partner-related services.

> *This can be thought of as the public face of the Service Portfolio.*

In some organizations, as the scope of Service Catalog continues to grow, we are seeing sales-related services, marketing services, financial services, and compliance services offered here to name a few. This is further testament to the unifying and transformational stature of Service Catalog. This provides support for our current topic of Service Portfolios in that the catalog brings a modern, friendly, and agile experience to the portfolio.

Figure 15.3 The Scope of Business Service Catalog

In the case of an organization with key audit and compliance services, the Business Service Catalog can be a valuable asset to provide a common, consistent, and central means by which to manage these services and the associated portfolio.

Increasingly, we are seeing organizations thinking of Service Portfolios and the associated Service Catalogs as a vehicle for planning and an operating engine that is a common platform for offering services. Beyond a view of the services themselves, we are extending Service Portfolios and the catalog to include cost. In the beginning it might simply be showing the cost of a service.

This cost visibility alone changes the expectations and behavior of the organization.

It creates understanding and it creates accountability. Even in the absence of cost tracking or a charging capability, the visibility of cost is a great place to start, and the charging mechanism can be added later. This comment applies to the internal model versus a customer-facing model where charging and billing might be necessary. For the very reasons Service Catalog is growing in adoption and visibility across IT and the organization, it is a natural platform for offering services to customers.

Are You Managing Service Portfolios Today?

Often the immediate answer I hear is "No." But let's answer a few questions to help us understand what's really happening:

1. Do you discuss and approve new services?
2. Do you build either an informal or a more formal business case before new services are approved?
3. Do you conduct any level of planning for future services that will be required for the business?
4. Do you retire services that are no longer used or adding value?
5. Do you maintain a list of all the services offered by IT today?

There are, of course, many other questions, but this is a good place to start. If the answer to most of these questions is "Yes," and it often is, then you are doing Service Portfolio

Management, even if it is a basic level or called by another name. It might not be structured or consistent, but the roots are there. As your IT Service Management practices continue to evolve, make a place for Service Portfolios for the reasons we touched on at the start of this chapter and use the structure outlined here as an aid to make progress. It is clear Service Portfolios will help enable world-class service delivery.

KEY INTEGRATIONS AND PARTNERSHIPS FOR SERVICE PORTFOLIOS

1. Service Catalog: teamwork and communication around both the strategy for both elements and in determining what services from the Service Portfolio should be offered through the catalog.

2. IT Leadership: the strategy for the Service Portfolio is critical to determining the services to be offered in the future, the services to be retired, and the general needs of services to support the evolution of the business.

3. Service Level Management: coordinate from the beginning service levels required for every service identified in the Service Portfolio. This must be seen as a natural and necessary part of the planning process for services.

4. Service Requests: liaison with the Service Request Managers to determine how and when each service in the portfolio will be offered to users and customers. Think of this as a commercial endeavor with a mind for how the target users will consume the service and how the service request process can help.

TIPS FOR SUCCESSFUL SERVICE PORTFOLIOS

5. Start simple. Build a single complete list of all active services. You will be surprised at the amount of discussion this activity creates.

6. Create a twelve- to twenty-four-month view of services under consideration for future launch.

7. Designate an owner for this process, a Service Portfolio advocate to work across the organization.

8. Require a complete business case for every candidate service, complete with costs, benefits, and resources required.

9. Leverage Service Catalog to drive visibility and improve delivery of the Services Portfolio.

10. Put structure to the trigger for the start of the Service Portfolio process and the ensuing complete sequence through to service retirement.

11. Take care to leverage a connection to the Financial Management process. This is all about aligning services with the business and managing investments.

CHAPTER 16

SERVICE AUTOMATION

Although not strictly an IT Service Management process as are the other twelve functions and processes highlighted throughout the pages of the book, the automation of service delivery is nonetheless critical to world-class IT Service Management today and is helping to reshape our future and what is possible. In recognizing the unique place Service Automation holds, we have dedicated this chapter to exploring this topic more completely. Service Automation today represents the confluence of several important elements:

1. A relentless drive for velocity in the business
2. New workflow technology
3. Rapidly growing customer expectations
4. The emergence of multi-channel support
5. Repeatable decision-making

Service Automation is unique in that it provides foundation support for most if not all of the twelve elements and the related extensions and IT strategies we review throughout the book. Put another way, Service Automation can make every IT Service Management process better.

A Relentless Drive for Velocity in the Business

A few themes are prominent throughout the book, with **speed** and **customer satisfaction** standing above all others. Although well understood, the word *satisfaction* does not really capture what we are in pursuit of. What we want to cultivate is a **thrilled** customer, a **loyal** customer, a customer who is **trusting** of the service, a customer whose expectations are consistently exceeded. In the storied past of Service Desk and Service Management, other factors have taken priority over raw speed. But our world has changed, and as we look to the future of world-class IT Service Management, **fast, faster, and fastest** will set the tone for everything we do!

There are a couple of important factors that are critical to customer happiness: me-level support and the consumerization of our service delivery models. These areas are explored in more detail within Chapter 20, The Consumerization of IT Service Management.

The opportunity for speed is everywhere.

We must adopt a ruthless and exhaustive search for ways in which we can shave seconds, minutes, hours, and even days from the average cycle time of our business processes both large and small. This encompasses time-based processes, including Incidents (Chapter 4), Service Requests (Chapter 5), Service Catalog (Chapter 6), Problem Management (Chapter 7), and Change Management (Chapter 11) to name a few. To drive velocity in the business, we need to begin by looking in the following places:

1. High-volume incident types
2. Common service requests
3. Long cycle-time business processes
4. Strategic business processes
5. Services with poor customer satisfaction

Our search for velocity should be incremental and iterative and be managed as a process that looks something like this:

Figure 16.1 The Programmatic Search for Speed

A few things to keep in mind when applying this model, or a variant of it, to your organization:

1. Expect to cycle through the model several times for a given business process or workflow.
2. Any and all time savings are good, be they large or small.
3. The sequence of this model should not be altered; streamline, simplify, and automate in that order and always in that order.
4. Our goal is a 90 percent reduction in cycle time with no reduction in customer/user satisfaction. This will most often be achieved in multiple steps, and there should be no expectation this can be accomplished in a single leap.
5. Don't be afraid to experiment with unconventional ideas. This can hold the key to some of the very best improvements. Never stop asking "Why?"

New Workflow Technology

We are truly fortunate to have access to technology that has seen a remarkable advancement in the past ten years. Our opportunity here is to leverage technology in order to practice world-class IT Service Management, and make no mistake, the right technology can help us achieve this primary goal. Some good examples include high-speed wireless Internet access, which is increasingly everywhere, smartphones with more robust apps, advanced Service Desk applications, social media, and VOIP solutions. While these examples are helping to reshape IT Service Management, this is only the beginning.

For this discussion we will focus on a key component of the current generation of IT Service Management applications: **workflow and business rules**. This technology is more than just a part of a Service Desk solution; it is strategic to what we are striving to elevate to world-class service delivery.

In the previous section we took a quick look at velocity in the business, and we proposed an iterative model for how to achieve our goal of a 90 percent reduction in cycle time for a business process. In this model, steps six and seven leverage automation and the forms this automation can take are business rules and workflow models. Business rules and a single entity can also be used as a building block in creating workflows which are multi-step, consisting of two or more actions.

Figure 16.2 Example Business Rule Structure

Think of this business rule object as a model for automating a stand-alone decision or action in the business. We use the term *business rule* because it is a good description of what this object does for us:

It defines and enforces a rule of how the business operates.

This business rule object can also be used as a building block in the construction of a multi-step workflow.

As a simple example, a business rule can detect that an incident has been closed, and an email notification is sent to the user and to the incident owner with the updated incident.

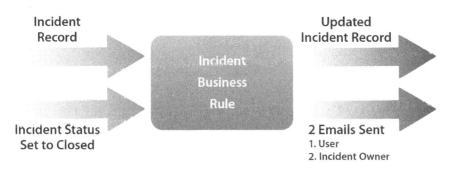

Figure 16.3 Example Incident Business Rule

This is a simple but very powerful model. This business rule is able to monitor all incidents (an unlimited number), and when any incident is closed, the necessary notification occurs instantly and without fail!

One advantage of the business rule (building block) and workflow model is scalability and reuse. We are able to create single business rules that can stand alone in some cases, and can be used as a component in a multi-step workflow. As an example, let's consider a single step in the Change Management process: "review a request for change."

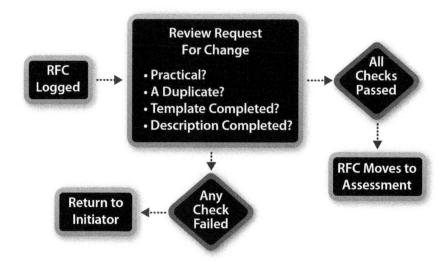

Figure 16.4 Request for Change Business Rule

This business rule captures the key checks for the review RFC stage in Change Management. If all four checks are passed, the RFC moves to the RFC assessment. If any of the four checks fail, the RFC is returned to the initiator.

To extend this model we now take a higher-level view of a workflow in which "review RFC" is a single step as follows:

Figure 16.5 Change Management Workflow

You can now see the power and strategic value of this decision object and workflow model. We are able to use technology to model a decision block and to model a business process that is then managed, monitored, and executed by way of an automated workflow. These business rules and workflow models can be as simple or complex as needed and become

a virtual partner in the business that removes the risk of human error while maximizing the speed of action.

Growing Customer Expectations

Throughout the book we cite a few cases of convergence that are reshaping the world in which we live. One such convergence is the coming together of highly competitive global markets and widely available high-speed Internet access which connects us to easy-to-use retail sites supported by secure electronic payment systems. One clear winner in this convergence is the customer, and a byproduct of this model is a shift in consumer behavior and in the expectations that come along with this shift.

Let's look at a simple example. Early this summer I decided to buy a new pair of trail shoes. Short on time as always, I decided to take advantage of good Wi-Fi on a flight from San Jose, CA, to Dallas, TX. I did a quick search and was able to access hundreds of reviews and ultimately narrow the many choices down to three brands. One brand is manufactured in Montana, one in Romania, and one in Germany. Several retailers offered all three brands on my short list, including one company I had used in the past with great results. In this case, I expected friendly customer service along with the option of phone or chat support to answer any questions I might have; fast shipping, including choices that are free; high-quality packaging so my stuff arrives undamaged; free returns in the event there is a problem with my order; and at checkout, several good payment options. The shoes arrived at my home before I did, fit perfectly, and looked great.

> *This experience is common today, but not so just a few years ago.*

Unreliable Internet access, a lack of trustworthy electronic payment methods, hard-to-use retail websites, and limited product choices made this experience slow and frustrating. Now, we expect fast and high- quality service every time. This pushes our expectations higher and higher, effectively creating a new generation of demanding and selfish customers. This is not a bad thing, but just the opposite; it is a very good thing. You have likely had similar experiences, and the bar continues to get higher as a result.

Make no mistake, brick-and-mortar purchasing will continue to have a place in today's culture as retailers recognize lingering security issues with online purchasing, but more importantly retailers

> *are focused on providing an in-store experience that is personal, memorable, enjoyable, and convenient.*

Now, you might be wondering what this has to do with IT Service Management and Service Automation? Great question. Our personal experiences and expectations as consumers are inextricably linked to our expectations in business. Our lofty expectations outside the office create a growing appetite for fast, personal, and outstanding service in the workplace, and this is the very mind-set of the users and customers we are serving on the Service Desk and extensions thereof. We explore this idea in more depth in Chapter 20, The Consumerization of IT Service Management, but it is included here because business rules, workflow modeling, and service automation are necessary and strategic tools that can be leveraged to meet and exceed growing customer expectations—**necessary** because we simply can't scale IT Service Management without good service automation, and **strategic** because we simply can't achieve world-class IT Service Management without the **speed** that robust service automation delivers.

Multi-Channel Support

The evolution and diversity of the channels through which we receive requests for and deliver a service are inescapable throughout the book and are addressed in Chapter 4 (Incidents), Chapter 5 (Service Requests), Chapter 6 (Service Catalog), Chapter 7 (Problem Management), and Chapter 16 (Service Automation). As such it is clear that the channels of support and central to IT Service Management, and only made possible through service automation.

In the beginning of the Help Desk, support was virtually single channel—the phone. While the phone remains by most counts the #1 single source of incidents for many organizations, and as high as 90 percent for some companies, the mix is changing like never before. At the heart of this are several key drivers:

1. Social media
2. Demand for 24X7 support
3. Self-Service
4. Service Catalog
5. VOIP/IVR tools

Service automation is a necessary foundation for the multi-channel support model to the degree that it is simply not possible without Service Desk automation. A multi-channel support model overview follows and, of course, includes the phone as one option:

Figure 16.6 Multi-Channel Support Model

This figure highlights the user/customer at the center of our support model (this is a great way to think every day), with traditional options available during standard manned Service Desk hours. Phone and walk-up support are foremost in the top and human part of this model, and these options will likely never go away completely. The biggest changes in this model are the 24X7 support channels shown in the lower half of Figure 16.6.

This is the fastest growing segment of support and was made possible largely by service automation.

It is true that email is not new, but what we can do with a simple email has changed remarkably. See Chapter 4 (Incidents) or Chapter 7 (Problem Management) for much more on this.

The other three 24X7 channels—Service Catalog, IVR, and Self-Service— are newer, leveraging advanced automation tools and carrying an increasing amount of the service request and incident volume. These three channels are exciting and powerful, truly changing the face and substance of IT into the future. So much so that we dedicate a full chapter to Service Catalog and include it among our Core 6 processes. For more of this good stuff, Self-Service and IVR are covered in Chapter 4 (Incidents).

A common characteristic of the four 24X7 support channels shown here (and others not shown here) is the degree to which these models leverage automation. In many cases these changes are fully automated and leverage the business rule building blocks and workflows described earlier in this chapter. The rapidly growing stature of these four channels is not an accident, and the four channels offer a few compelling benefits:

1. Fast—90 percent time savings in delivering a service is possible
2. Always available
3. Simple, friendly user experience

4. Cost effective—80 percent cost savings versus a live analyst interaction
5. Scalable, can support thousands of concurrent users

This multi-channel model is a case where we see both strong tactical benefits and strategic value.

Repeatable Decision-Making

A natural upside of service automation is the absolute and unfailing consistency we see from the decision-making models. There is certainly an initial investment of time from our human experts in order to build the business rule and workflow templates and capture what our best people know. However, this investment of time pays back to the organization many times over when the automation tools are put into daily use and we begin to appreciate the 100 percent consistent and 100 percent reliable actions and decision support that is provided by Service Automation. And we get the added benefit of business rule triggers and time models that ensure not a second is wasted when moving through the steps of a business process.

In the case of best practices, including ITIL, service automation enables a tailored and precise description of the best practices templates (incident, problem, and change are good examples), some of which can be very complex. Once captured, these templates are then leveraged by the business every day and bring us closer to world-class performance.

TIPS FOR SUCCESSFUL SERVICE AUTOMATION

1. Utilize a structured approach to automation. Figure 16.1 provides a framework to start with. Although it is the easiest, a purely random or opportunistic approach will not yield the best results and will greatly slow progress.
2. Have quantified goals defined for every automation project. We are not automating for automation's sake.
3. Before attempting to automate a business process with a workflow model, name an expert in the business to be the process mentor.
4. If not in place today, build a plan to deliver the 24X7 support channels in Figure 16.6. If only one is possible, start with Service Catalog.
5. Remember, our primary goal is speed! Velocity unlocks unlimited value in the business and is foremost in our pursuit of world-class IT Service Management.

CHAPTER 17

ENTERPRISE SERVICE MANAGEMENT

In the past decade we have seen a spike in the demand for Service Management solutions that don't fit the mold of the traditional IT Service Desk. This need originates in organizations outside IT—human resources, customer service, facilities, finance, and marketing to name a few. Because these organizations are non-IT but the requirements are very much about managing services across the business and service delivery, we commonly use the term Enterprise Service Management (ESM) to describe this spinoff of the traditional IT Service Management model.

Characteristics of ESM include:

1. Offering a service to a group of users or customers that will not necessarily be delivered by the IT organization and could be delivered by multiple organizations in partnership with IT.
2. The ESM model does not focus on incidents and is not limited to the corresponding Break/Fix focus.

3. The ESM experience is more business-oriented and less technical than ITSM.

4. In the scope of what I have addressed in this book, ESM is well served by the Service Request, Service Catalog, and Service Automation processes and capabilities.

5. Service Catalog is a good natural fit for the offering of ESM services.

6. An ESM offering is normally a very specific service that is delivered in a simple model that does not require IT resources to manage the process.

7. We can think of ESM as a business service, delivered to business people by business people.

8. ESM has had a positive influence on IT Service Desk, resulting in a warmer and friendlier IT experience, including Incident Management.

9. ESM makes good use of service automation tools, as simplicity and a quick response are a priority.

10. Many IT best practices, although certainly not all, have proven to be a good fit for ESM.

Enterprise Service Management is a fun topic to kick around because it is a great example of why the star of IT is rising in the organization.

> *After laboring in relative anonymity for decades, the business is now turning to IT for help with delivering services of all kinds.*

The timing is good because IT is ready and able to help for a number of reasons:

1. IT Service Management tools have matured and are proven over thirty years of market changes.
2. The significant pressures and accountability of audit, compliance, and corporate governance have strengthened and accelerated the evolution of IT Service Management.
3. Other business tools, including CRM, Call Center, and ERP, have not achieved the same level of sophistication and have left the business looking for alternative solutions.
4. IT best practices have proven to translate well for improving non-IT service delivery.
5. The core elements and software tools that enable Self- Service, Service Catalog, workflow, and service requests adapt quickly to support Enterprise Service delivery.

To help bring all this together, we will look at three examples of Enterprise Service Management in action, in support of services that occur in most organizations every day.

Example #1: Booking a Conference Room

Reserving a conference room for a meeting or other small group or large group activity occurs every day in most organizations. In some cases, demand for conference rooms is high, and preferred rooms are booked well into the future. Rooms with video conferencing, high seating capacity, or other unique resource can create an entire cultural phenomenon of competition. While it is certainly possible to schedule a meeting room with a simple calendar application, organizations are recognizing there are some advantages to managing these rooms with an Enterprise Service Management model:

1. Submitting a service request can be fast and simple but at the same time capture a good profile of the true requirement.
2. Service automation can automate many of the steps in an otherwise manual process.
3. Should conflicts arise, and they often do, a good application can quickly evaluate the competing requests and find a solution.
4. The automation, including integration to third party applications, element of ESM can track the costs associated with these activities, track the organizations making the request, and perform an analysis of capacity requirements.
5. The ESM model provides a central collection point for these requests and enables reporting and trending.

There is a lot to like about this model versus simply scheduling meetings on an Outlook calendar. ESM brings us the advantages of speed, automation, and the understanding of demand and the ability to effectively plan for the future.

The process begins with a meeting request form, often found in the Service Catalog:

Date:

Meeting Name:

Requester:

Start Date and Time:

End Date and Time:

First Room Choice:

Second Room Choice:

Special Requests and Comments:

Requester Email:

Figure 17.1 Example Meeting Request Form

The completed request is submitted, which then triggers the automated workflow to begin.

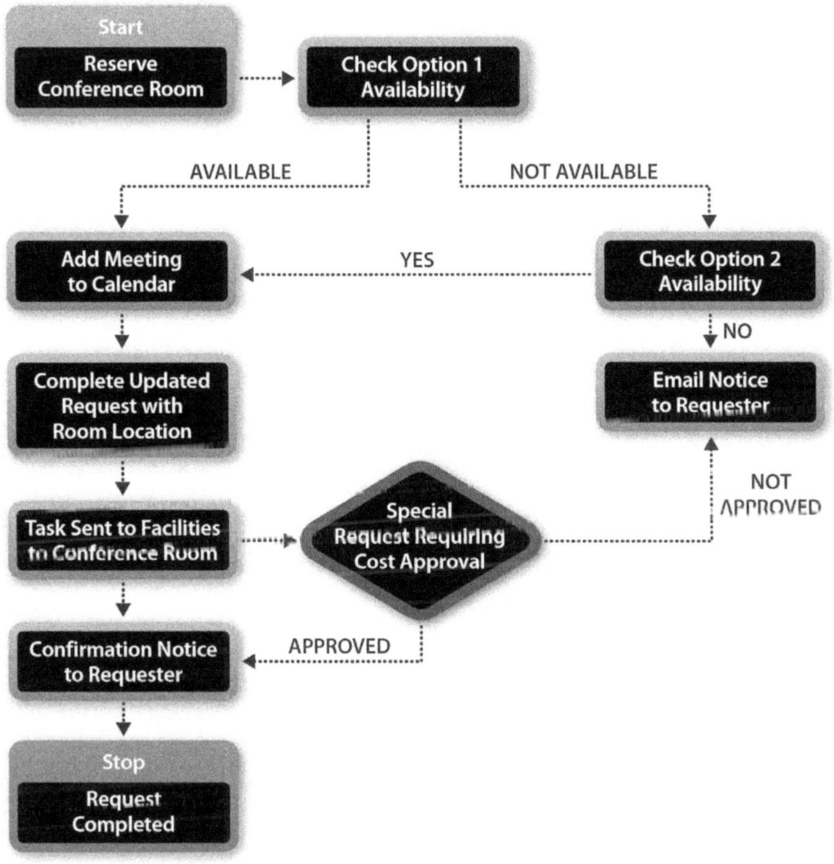

Figure 17.1 Workflow Overview of Conference Room Booking

At a count of ten elements, this is not a complex workflow nor should it be to reserve a conference room. Although somewhat simple, it does illustrate the case of a set of tasks and checks that occur in the organization in support of this request, and it can be executed quickly and consistently following all the governing business rules. In your organization there might be additional steps that are necessary, and this model can be adapted as needed.

This is another reminder of how we can leverage the service automation model we covered in Chapter 16. I have made the point about speed many times, and this is an exciting benefit of automating a business process such as this. Yet another benefit is the ability to scale as the volume of requests grows.

> *A good workflow engine will always keep up and execute the right steps in the right order every time.*

This keeps the business moving and allows our people to focus on the important things and not get distracted by a cumbersome manual process. This can be very energizing to the organization—the ability to count on an advanced application to assist in doing our jobs better every day, offload the administrative and repetitive tasks, and take comfort they will be done correctly. We also get the added benefit of central tracking and archiving of requests for future review. This is a beautiful thing.

Example #2: Off-boarding An Employee

In this second example we will take a look at a broader process and another process that is common in many businesses. The off-boarding of an employee requires cross-functional coordination of multiple tasks governed by multiple business rules. All in all a good case of ESM at work.

We begin with a service request that can originate in Service Catalog, a Web Portal, or from some other front end. Expect these sources of a service request to continue to evolve as we find faster, easier, and more convenient methods to collect this information from a customer while continuing to improve the customer experience. This pursuit never really ends.

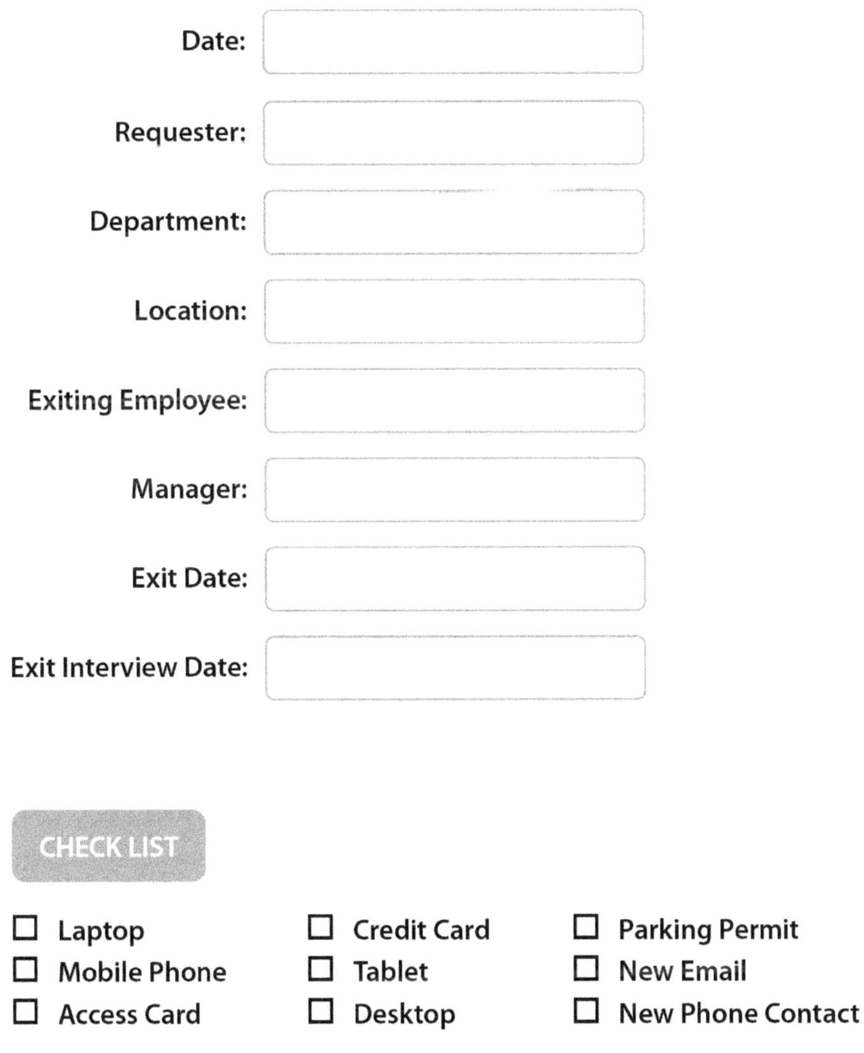

Date:	
Requester:	
Department:	
Location:	
Exiting Employee:	
Manager:	
Exit Date:	
Exit Interview Date:	

CHECK LIST

- ☐ Laptop
- ☐ Mobile Phone
- ☐ Access Card

- ☐ Credit Card
- ☐ Tablet
- ☐ Desktop

- ☐ Parking Permit
- ☐ New Email
- ☐ New Phone Contact

Figure 17.3 Employee Off-boarding Request Form

This request requires more information than what we saw with the conference room request, but the more sophisticated applications in the market today use pull-downs and pre-populated fields/matching to simplify the process and save time.

When the request is submitted, the workflow is triggered:

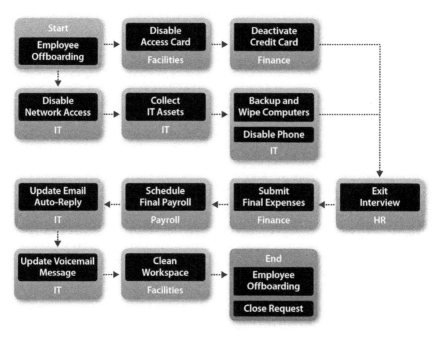

Figure 17.4 Example Off-boarding Workflow Model

We can leverage a high degree of automation to schedule and coordinate the activities. This will ensure wasted time is minimized, each step occurs in the proper sequence, and each participating organization is notified and prepared to execute the appropriate task. To the point of this being very much a cross-functional business process, we have the following organizations participating:

1. Employee's manager starts the process
2. Facilities
3. Finance
4. HR
5. IT
6. Payroll

With the number of teams involved in the sequence of events, it is easy to see why the traditional manual method can be disjointed and result in misunderstandings and delays. Due to these same challenges, ESM is a great solution and transforms this workflow from problematic to highly efficient.

Example #3: Launch A Marketing Campaign

I included this example because it is very different from the first two, giving us a more complete and diverse set of three examples. It is also a great illustration of how ESM is spreading throughout the organization and shattering many of the traditional views of service delivery.

This is a testament to the flexibility and adaptability of the core IT Service Management models. The marketing service request looks something like this:

Date:

Requester:

Organization or Cost Code:

Campaign Name:

Budget Requested:

Budget Approved:

Vendors and Agencies:

Launch Date:

Comments:

**Figure 17.5 Marketing Campaign
Service Request Form**

This process can be initiated with a streamlined request, as the intent is a bit different than for examples #1 and #2. In this case we are trying to create better visibility and account-ability of the expenses and activities associated with a mar-keting campaign. A marketing campaign commits company resources, bandwidth, and intellectual focus to a project that might run for an extended period of time. These are impor-tant initiatives, and managing the launch and lifecycle of a campaign within an ESM solution helps to get the most from our investment in a marketing program where

more traditional methods for tracking these campaigns are ill equipped to pro-vide the information and detail needed to fully understand what is being committed to bring the campaign to life and to oper-ate the campaign successfully.

The request creates an event in the business that gives us a baseline for the campaign timeline. The Date field, Requester, and Organization give us the desired start date, and the cam-paign owner will then answer any questions and coordinate activities. The Budget Requested and Budget Approved allow us to verify the financial approvals are in place, and if not to request the approval before activities are scheduled and re-sources committed. This helps to avoid the waste that occurs with false starts or the confusion created when marketing activities are not coordinated with finance for the budgeting, PO, and vendor payment activities to name a few.

Many marketing campaigns include contractors, consul-tants, agencies, and vendors, so we need to have visibility of these companies from the start.

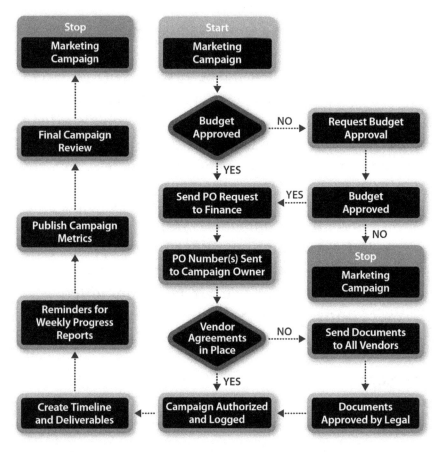

Figure 17.6 Marketing Campaign Workflow

The anatomy of a marketing campaign varies greatly from organization to organization, so your process will likely look a bit different—but you get the idea.

This is intended to illustrate a business activity that is very much non-IT and how we can put some structure to the series of activities that occur, the timing and dependencies of these activities, and design into the process the checks and balances that are so important. While non-IT processes and data may not be subject to the same compliance and audit standards as IT, many of the same principles apply and create the opportunity to significantly improve performance.

This has far-reaching implications and can create a more competitive and differentiated business model and breed confidence and passion in everything we do.

I would take this a step further and make the claim that world-class IT Service Management creates a cultural shift that inevitably extends far beyond IT and into every organization and aspect of the business. In this very real manner, IT becomes an engine of business process innovation and truly today, realizing the vision we felt was within our reach for the past decade of IT becoming a strategic partner to the business and leading the organization into the future. We devote more time to the cultural discussion in Chapter 20 (A Culture of Excellence). You might be wondering what culture has to do with IT and with IT Service Management. It has everything to do with world-class IT Service Management! As much and likely more so than processes, tools, and technology.

And therein lies one of the central themes to the book. Anybody can run a Service Desk and deliver services to an organization. This is easy.

The journey to world-class IT Service Management is fundamentally rooted in culture, attitude, passion, and focus.

Make no mistake, we need strong technology and sound processes, but without the right culture and people in place, what we have is just another Service Desk. Perhaps good, but not great. I can't make this point emphatically enough, so forgive the repeated references to this *purest ray serene* that guides our journey.

To close out on the topic of Enterprise Service Management, we should look beyond our three examples to recognize how a strong IT Service Management model enables ESM:

1. A flexible service request model can accommodate virtually any enterprise request.
2. The Service Catalog or Self-Service experience can be shared to offer a friendly entry to the customer or employee.
3. The tools of Service Automation quickly adapt to enable the complete and accurate capture of just about any business workflow.
4. A reporting and integration framework common in the best ITSM applications allows us to generate reports and integrate with other business systems, including ERP, CRM, HR, and finance/payroll as needed.

While it has had an undeniable impact on business today and has earned our attention throughout this chapter, in many ways ESM remains in its infancy. Looking at its trajectory, we expect to see the continued growth and evolution of ESM over the next decade and beyond, all while making good use of the models that have matured in support of the Service Desk over the past thirty years.

CHAPTER 18

THE CONSUMERIZATION OF IT SERVICE MANAGEMENT

IT and Service Management are being influenced and re-shaped by multiple forces, including the Internet experience, social media, online commerce, mobile devices, and much more. One byproduct of these forces is the convergence of personal and professional behaviors and expectations that will accelerate the evolution of everything we do and the strategy that will drive IT Service Management models of the future. It has taken some time, but we are now seeing clear inroads of these influences across the IT organizations, one of the last strongholds of traditional business.

Characteristics of this evolution and influence include:

1. Everything happens fast.
2. 24X7 access is assumed.

3. The experience must be personal.
4. Access is possible with any device.
5. No human is needed on the other side.
6. It is easy to do what I need.
7. No waiting.
8. The user is in complete control.

For the sake of this discussion and to also capture the essence of what is happening in this rebirth, let's refer to the model as "Me-Level Support." This model is optimized, not sub-optimal, for the individual. Simply said, but a lot is implied. This is a significant departure from the traditional IT models of the past and should not be overlooked as a dramatic and meaningful change.

Think of this experience as the best of the Service Desk, in an experience that is fast, friendly, and personal. Me-Level Support looks something like this:

Figure 18.1 Me-Level Support

This model can only become a reality when leveraging the best tools from IT (user experience building blocks, knowledge, workflow, mobility, and more) and put to work to serve the demanding, impatient, and selfish knowledge worker who understands a new paradigm:

1. The phone is very inefficient for many tasks.
2. Immediate gratification is expected.
3. It must be easy.
4. More and more work is done on a mobile device.

5. Remember who I am and let me do everything my way.
6. Has to be really fast.
7. Everything needs to work around the clock.

From this model emerges many new realities, including the phone becoming a specialized tool. This is a big departure from the past thirty years where the phone was the daily standard. Today, it is just too slow. The new normal is web, Self-Service, and Service Catalog. Email is okay, but it also is increasingly limiting.

Taking this line of thought further, let's look at an example of a common employee request from IT:

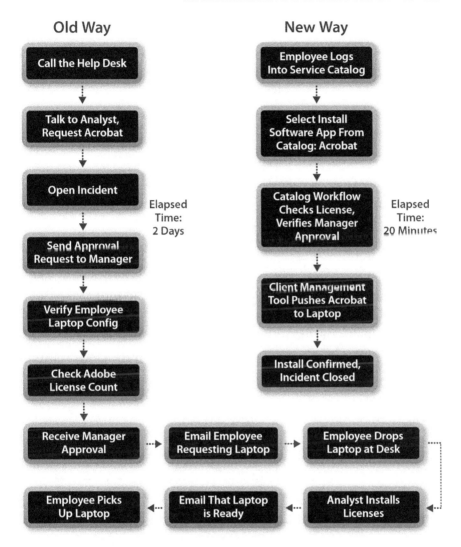

**Figure 18.2 Request the Installation
of Software On My Computer**

What this example highlights is the strategic value of this new consumerized model—extreme speed! This velocity unlocks tremendous potential for improvements across the organization. With speed, many things become possible: time to think and time to find a better way.

> ***Given the chance, good people will natu-***
> ***rally find a path to working smarter, and***
> ***the gift of speed provides the opportunity***
> ***to discover that path.***

This would simply not be possible without precious time. Speed is the great enabler. Speed saves money, speed creates opportunity, speed makes people heroes, speed exceeds expectations, and speed can give rise to the ultimate competitive differentiation.

With the context of the Me-Level Support model in Figure 18.1, let's take a closer look at each of the eight elements that make up this model. They each have a story to tell, and this is just the beginning of a makeover we will see reshape IT over the next ten years. If you have read more than just a few pages of this book, you won't be at all surprised where we start.

Fast

In the delivery of world-class IT Service Management, there is no greater value than that made possible by speed. It is important to recognize that the value created by speed is not limited to speed itself, which is very important, of course, but this value is in fact multiplied by the additional opportunities created by speed, including the creation of time to ask and answer the following questions:

1. What new services should we offer to our customers?
2. How can we improve the services we are offering today?

3. How can we win new customers?
4. How can we further reduce the average fulfillment time of existing services?
5. If customers are not using our service, why?
6. If our customers would have us do one thing better or differently, what would that be?

The balance we are trying to create here is one of:

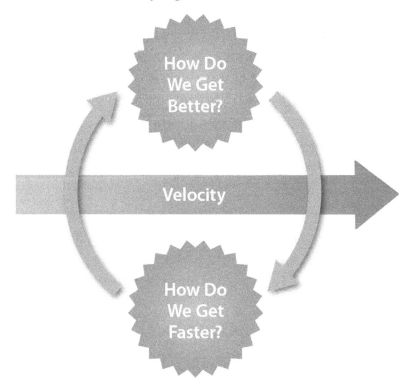

Figure 18.3 The Balance of Better and Faster

These two factors are partners in greatness. They also naturally complement each other and create a culture that never stops searching and fighting for ways to deliver a more valuable service.

24X7

The clock for business has changed. Gone forever is the idea that we can deliver service during normal business hours and that is good enough.

In many ways the idea of normal business hours is obsolete with our world-class IT Service Management paradigm.

This paradigm is a completely different model. Our hours of operation are not anything like 8:00 a.m. to 5:00 p.m., but rather anytime the customer needs something. This is a very simple and powerful model that is reshaping the future of IT and the future of Service Management. Think about it. When we start with this, it changes everything. We can't expect users to shape their behavior and needs to the hours of the Service Desk or the availability of a service. This is backward. We need to think in terms of how do we make every service available when our customers need it? To be great, 24X7 is no longer an option—it is a necessity.

Person or No Person

In some cases, speaking with a live agent is exactly what we need and enables the best possible experience. In other cases it is not necessary and simply slows us down. Because no one model is the answer, the key here is choice. Me-Level Support anticipates the agent requirement and makes speaking with an agent fast and convenient. Note that in this case we must arm the agent with the right information in order to provide a great experience for the user or customer, and the leading VOIP/IVR/Screen Pop tools are outstanding in this regard. Chat and phone are two good options for the live model. In the case of no-person-required, we can leverage the Self-Service, Service Catalog, email and voice automation tools described in detail within the chapters on Incidents, Service Catalog, and Service Automation. We should fully expect new options to emerge in the years ahead.

The key here is flexibility. The choice of the user/customer should not be assumed and will always be changing. If we design in this flexibility from the beginning, then we are well equipped to take on any changes that lie ahead. If we assume this consumerized Me-Level Support model must be delivered through a person exclusively, or through automated no-person channels exclusively, then we have diminished the power of the model. Assume change will happen and will never stop.

Personal

A fundamental shift occurring in Service Management today is born of our pursuit of world-class service models and of the consumerization influences we address in this chapter. This shift is a realignment of our value index and one that now focuses on speed and customer happiness above efficiencies and savings. Let's be clear, efficiencies and cost savings continue to have a place in IT operations and in IT Service Management, but we now understand that speed and a thrilled customer can fundamentally change the business and drive strategic value originating from IT. This is our foremost focus in world-class IT Service Management.

A personal experience is at the intersection of both the consumerization of IT and the creation of a happy and loyal customer.

In many ways, the genesis of this consumerized service model can be traced back to Service Management and the Service Desk. This concept and strategy will reshape all of what we do in IT. A personal experience includes a few key things:

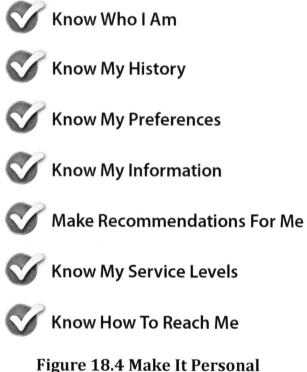

Figure 18.4 Make It Personal

What makes Me-Level Support so powerful is the combination of these eight factors while making it personal. This ensures that every service interaction is the best it can be and we are cultivating world-class service one experience and one customer at a time.

Adaptable

Change is a reality today in virtually every business. The collision of the powerful forces we have referenced—including the Internet, social media, online shopping, and global competition, along with our increasing reliance on new technologies and our constant companion, the smartphone—is reshaping everything we do in business and in IT Service Management.

The world-class IT Service Management organization will experience an evolutionary improvement with the following principles and mind-set:

 **Recognize the Unstoppable Momentum of Change**

Plan For Change In Everything We Do

 **Create A Culture That Embraces Change**

Build Business Models That Allow the Organization To Thrive With Change

Figure 18.5 The Evolution of Service Organizations

Today, many organizations have not yet gone beyond step #1 to #2 but that will change.

Good to great Service Desks are at stage #2 or #3. The very best teams are in, or close to operating in, stage #4. This changes everything, and is only possible if we are providing Me-Level Support and have an adaptable process. With a Service Desk designed to be adaptable and anticipate change, we are able to make the necessary shift when change occurs and in a manner that is swift, with minimal cost, and with little disruption. This change can take many forms, but with some thoughtful planning, we can adapt as needed. This is very much about mind-set and culture.

Easy

We all love easy. This is at the center of the consumerization of IT Service Management.

> *Easy adds value, easy makes customers happy, easy saves time, and easy ultimately makes world-class possible.*

That does not mean that world-class = easy. If only it were that simple. It means that easy is essential to world-class performance, in combination with a few other factors, and that world-class performance is not possible if we have core services that are difficult to request or deliver.

> *The thing about easy is that it is not easy!*

It is certainly a simple concept, but great effort must be invested to make easy a reality. For this to occur we must understand what our users and customers need and then determine how we can meet this need in the simplest, quickest, and most satisfying manner.

What this means for IT Service Management is that we must make it easy to request a service, to get an update on a request, to get a question answered, or to report an issue—all the things our employees and customers do every day. Me-Level Support does not work if our common needs are difficult, frustrating, complicated, and slow. This is, of course, the antithesis of world-class.

The consumerization of IT calls attention to a set of principles that unfortunately have not always been embraced by IT and by the Service Desk. That is changing now and it is very exciting—the eight principles of Me-Level Support capture not only the spirit of this consumerization of how we deliver service, but affects everything we do in Service Management and our baseline for world-class performance, world-class Service Management, and a world-class business.

Any Device

The increasing power and convenience of mobile devices has made this our preferred platform for everything we do.

Mobile devices have both blurred and moved the lines of the past between our job and our personal life.

Phone calls, email, app usage, Internet browsing, texting,

and social media access are all smashed together in an "always on" model that reflects how we live our lives.

This translates into a requirement for how we expect to access Service Management tools as an analyst, and how a user or customer expects to access a service.

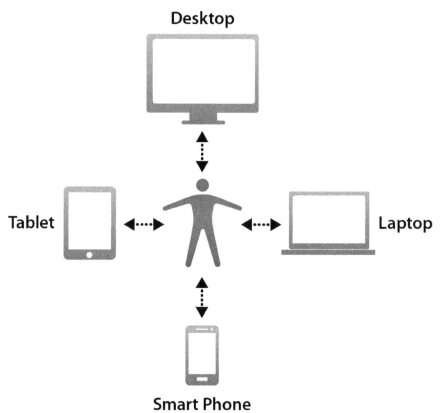

Figure 18.6 Devices and People

This expectation and the related lifestyle behavior are very much a product of the consumerization of IT. On a related note, this is also driving the explosion of endpoints in the business, which, in turn, creates a greater need for processes, including Change Management and Configuration Management.

The theme throughout this chapter is clear—users expect immediate gratification, meaning fast and easy above all else. This is ultimately a good thing because this expectation is reshaping IT and accelerating the business going forward. We should recognize that this evolution of devices will not stop with the tablet and smartphone.

> *A new generation of device will appear on the market in the next five to ten years that will change, yet again, our expectations and standards in both how we live and how we work.*

This is an opportunity to both serve and to be served better than ever before. This is at the heart of IT Service Management.

Automated

Automation is inextricably linked to two of our key consumerization principles—**fast and easy**. Yes, fast and easy again!

While we all agree that fast and easy are very good goals, we simply can't deliver this experience without automation. I felt the Automation of Service Management important enough that it earned a full chapter, Chapter 19.

For the delivery of a consumerized IT experience, automation is leveraged to work behind the scenes in order to bring to life the model in Figure 18.1. As a quick review, we should remember why automation is so powerful:

1. Fast
2. Always ready
3. Remembers who I am
4. Consistent
5. Accurate

Yes, this is an awesome model. But it is important to recognize that all this good stuff does not come for nothing. The Service Desk must do the work to fully understand the needs of the user or customer, to then translate these needs into the configuration of the automated components, and to then ensure the automation is operating properly.

The **leverage** we get with automation is that once the initial investment is made to capture the needs of the user and properly configure business rules and workflows, this automated experience works on our behalf all day, every day, and does not make mistakes or slow down.

> *Automation is a beautiful thing, and a key engine to making Me-Level Support a reality.*

The example of Me-Level Support referenced for this discussion is certainly not the full extent of the consumerization of IT. It does, however, embody many of the key concepts that capture why this force is so transformational. At the same time, expect to see Me-Level Support offered by a growing number of organizations and a necessary Service Desk function in order to realize the vision of world-class IT Service Management.

CHAPTER 19

MAKING SENSE OF CLOUD AND ON PREMISES

The impact of cloud and Software as a Service (SaaS) on the IT Service Management market over the past ten years is undeniable. However, like many large forces that reshape a market, there has been a great deal of hype, confusion, and misleading information surrounding these technologies and the associated operating and deployment models.

Today, approximately fifteen percent of Service Desks are utilizing SaaS, and new purchases of IT Service Management applications are trending at 70-80 percent. We expect this trend to continue over the next three to five years, and the longer term trending is not yet clear.

To establish a basic definition, cloud solutions are delivered to user devices, normally a laptop computer, desktop computer, tablet, or mobile phone on demand and utilize the Internet as a primary resource. This service is delivered by a service provider that is managing the application and data on behalf of the client and in a data center that utilizes a pool of shared resources to gain economies of scale. The resources within these data centers can be configured and provisioned quickly to meet the changing demands of customers. In most cases the user simply needs a capable device and a browser to access the service.

The on-premises model (commonly referred to as on premise or simply premise) has been the primary access model for the past twenty-five years and continues to represent approximately eighty-five percent of usage today. This model requires software to be installed locally on premise and on computing resources in the client environment and under local management along with all user data.

While the data shows that SaaS has seen undeniable growth and has some compelling benefits, this model is not for every organization. In order to shed some light on these options and to get past the swirl of information, both good and bad, surrounding cloud and premise,

we will take a fact-based and analytical approach to helping an organization determine if cloud or premise is the best fit for their profile of requirements.

This is intended to first help you understand the characteristics of each model for a Service Management solution, and then to help you self-diagnose which deployment model is the best fit for the unique needs of any organization.

For the remainder of this chapter, we will look at **ten key**

areas that can help profile the organization and offer insights to your natural fit to a set of key requirements.

Cloud	Premise
• Year 1 Costs Favor Cloud	• Long Term TCO Can Favor Premise
• Save Money on Infrastructure	• Overall Consulting Costs Similar
• Annual Subscription Model	• Includes Perpetual License

Figure 19.1 Year One Costs Versus Five-Year TCO

Our first issue explores an organization's appetite for saving money in the short term. Cloud normally provides savings in the first one to three years, versus the desire to focus on a longer term TCO, which will favor premise. While there is some information in the market that suggests cloud saves money in both cases, a careful review of the facts shows this is simply not true. The basic characteristics of the annual subscription versus a perpetual license model will support the summary shown in Figure 19.1.

Cloud	Premise
• Lowers Requirement for IT Services	• Will Require IT Support
• Data and Application in Vendor Data Center	• Data and Application are Local
• Upgrades Managed by Vendor	• Upgrades are Do-It-Yourself

Figure 19.2 Current State of IT Resources

Our second issue takes a look at the state of IT resources available in the organization, recognizing the cloud and premise models are very different in this regard. The cloud model reduces the need for local IT resources as many of the application and data management responsibilities are taken on by the service provider. This is a characteristic of cloud that is attractive for many. The premise model will require IT support for both the initial installation and for upgrades. Some organizations do have strong IT resources, and this is not a problem and can be an advantage. The premise model does provide more control, given the right IT resources as both the application and the data will be resident locally, which can be a plus for premise.

- Other Cloud Apps in Place
- Cloud Well Understood
- Executive Support for Cloud

- No Cloud Apps in Business
- CRM and ERP are Premise Today
- Management Sees Cloud as Risk

Figure 19.3 Current Experience with Cloud

The third issue explores the organization's current aptitude for cloud. Often overlooked, this is an issue that needs to be considered. More than just a technology or a deployment model, cloud creates cultural change and much more. If cloud is currently used in other areas (CRM and ERP are the two examples we use here), many of these cultural and organizational adjustments have been made and the risk is reduced. If cloud is not currently used in other areas and the Service Desk will be a pioneer in this regard, the risk becomes much greater. This should not be taken to imply the project will fail. It does, however, need to be understood and not underestimated. This is not a small matter.

- Location of Data Center Can Be Significant
- Data Center Security is Increasingly Accepted But Not Universal
- Some Regulations Extend to Data Center Personnel

- On-Site Data Can Be a Requirement
- Regulations Must Be Addressed by IT Team
- Provides More Testing and Procedural Flexibility

Figure 19.4 Security and Governance Regulations

The fourth issue raises some significant and potentially complex issues related to security and governance. One example that is very much at the center of many related discussions is data sovereignty. This is a global matter, and the requirements and standards of countries continue to evolve; we simply don't know many of the answers today. At a high level, the requirements around data sovereignty can vary from country to country and can place requirements on both the location and the management processes of the data center and the operations personnel. It is important to recognize this issue up front, to get the facts on what is required for your organization, including the location of the users, and to then plan accordingly.

Cloud	Premise
• Limited Number of Integrations	• Larger Number of Integrations
• Well Defined and Understood	• Evolving and Complex
• Typically Static/One-Way	• Dynamic and Bi-Directional

Figure 19.5 System Integrations

Most IT Service Management solutions will include a number of integrations with other systems in order to complete the full scope of work required for all processes. These integrations can include but will not be limited to event monitoring, asset discovery, ERP, employee authentication, compliance, and CRM systems. The integration models for cloud and premise can be very different, and this model must be aligned with what the business will require. In general terms, a large number of complex and dynamic integrations are potentially problematic for cloud and will be better aligned with premise. Cloud does well with a smaller number of integrations that are more static in nature and not subject to change. In many ways we are simply trying to gauge risk as there are no real absolutes in the areas we are reviewing. It is always a good strategy to first understand and then calibrate risk in order to maximize the opportunity for success. System integrations are one such area.

Cloud

Premise

Cloud	Premise
• Poor History With Upgrades	• Good History with Upgrades
• No Proven Upgrade Process	• Mature Upgrade Process
• Lacking In-House Skills	• The Right Skills in IT

Figure 19.6 History With Application Upgrades

In the premise model all upgrades must be managed and delivered by the IT organization and executed locally. With cloud, upgrades are managed and delivered by the service provider. This is a large contrast that should be understood upfront but surprisingly another area that is often overlooked. This is neither good nor bad and must be taken in the context of the upgrade history of the organization. Some organizations are skilled at upgrades and have a strong history with upgrade success. These organizations likely have an upgrade methodology proven and defined over the course of many historical upgrades and are confident in delivering upgrades to the organization on a schedule controlled fully from the inside. Other organizations have a poor history with upgrades and simply don't have the processes, skills, or people to take on the responsibility of managing upgrades for success into the future. These organizations will be more likely to embrace the standardized upgrade model offered by the cloud service. Which are you?

• Organization Ready to Embrace
  Standard Apps
• Business is More Standardized
• Bad Experiences with Custom Apps

• Apps Tend to be More Customized
• Business is Highly Unique
• Aptitude to Sustain Customizations

Figure 19.7 Readiness for "Out-of-the-Box"

The growing maturity of IT Service Management has provided the market with a much more complete and proven set of best practices and implementation models. This in turn has made an out-of-the-box approach to implementation more feasible than ever before. However, even with this progress there remains a group of organizations that operate a more unique or highly configured set of processes and workflow models that make it more difficult to adopt standard out-of-the-box solutions. The cloud model can thrive when the organization operates in a manner that is accommodated by standard models but will be challenged to be successful over time for those organizations with more unique requirements or requirements that are rapidly evolving and changing. One approach to better understand the fit, or lack thereof, is running a Proof of Concept (POC) exercise, which will take a set of key business processes and have them modeled in the cloud or premise application and then evaluated by key business owners who are experts in the selected POC models. Normally it will be clear, when evaluating these example business processes in the cloud or premise application, if the fit provided is acceptable. It is especially important to understand a couple of things during this process: how much time is required to enable the selected business processes and how much effort is required to make changes to the application should these business processes change in the future, recognizing that they always do.

• Growth Through M&A	• Linear Organic Growth
• Periods of High Growth	• Track Record of Predictable Expansion
• Growth Tends to Be More Distributed	• Growth Tends to be More Centralized/Consolidated

Figure 19.8 Corporate Development Model

The nature of corporate development can have an influence on the selection of cloud or premise. This might not be an obvious area to explore, so let's take a closer look. If an organization has a history of mergers and acquisitions, has experienced periods of high growth or the organic growth has occurred at multiple locations, a cloud-based deployment can make a lot of sense. In this case, we can be supporting a corporate consolidation or standardization initiative that is bringing users from legacy and often multiple disparate systems onto a single platform and application. This creates an opportunity to create a corporate standard, consistency, and synergy across multiple divisions or operating units. In the case of more linear growth and a traditional expansion model built around a single or a smaller number of corporate centers, this organization is a good candidate for a premise deployment. These organizations are more likely to have more standardized and mature systems in place, which creates the opportunity to move forward onto an improved and scalable solution in unison. As is the case with each of the ten areas we explore, there can be exceptions, but for most organizations this characterization will hold.

- Moderately to Highly Distributed
- More Complex Upgrade Process
- Reliable Web Access

- Users Are More Centralized
- Upgrades More Localized
- High Quality Services/Infrastructure

Figure 19.9 User Distribution

This ninth area complements what we reviewed in the previous area. A corporate organizational model that has users highly distributed and in many cases lacking the necessary corporate technology and infrastructure as a result can often be supported effectively with a cloud deployment. Cloud enables these users to operate efficiently with very little local resource by accessing the IT Service Management service over the Internet and from their computer or mobile phone. Reliable and high-speed web access is required for this model.

In the case of a corporate organizational model that has users more centrally located in larger corporate offices and with more localized and concentrated resources, including IT capacity, this can be a better fit for a premise deployment. The responsibilities that come along with this model would include managing user data locally and installing and managing the IT Service Management solution on a local server, which then makes the application available to users over the corporate intranet. The associated security and upgrades are also managed locally by IT. Very different models, but both can be equally effective. It then becomes a matter of evaluating the state of your organization and fitting the right deployment model to the specific needs of the business.

One further thought on this is to mix the deployment models across the business, where one segment of the organization can be supported with a cloud service and another can be supported with a premise system, bringing the best of both worlds to the business. This third model is a good option to consider if needed.

- Op Ex
- Reduced Year 1 Expense
- Can Be Beneficial to Cash Flow
- Some Exposure to Annual Increases

- Cap Ex
- Larger Year 1 Expense
- May Require Additional Assets
- More Predictability Year-Over-Year

**Figure 19.10 Capital Expense
versus Operating Expense Budgets**

In this tenth area we explore a financial consideration that will be relevant to the CFO and the expenses associated with the IT Service Management solution. In some cases, decisions are driven by this consideration alone, so its importance should not be underestimated.

The annual subscription associated with a cloud service will be allocated as operating expense, whereas the perpetual license purchase associated with a premise solution will be treated as capital expense. The current state of budgets varies greatly from organization to organization, but this becomes an issue as in some cases the availability of operating expense will exceed that of capital expense. This can favor the cloud model. In other cases, capital expense is available and must be spent within a fiscal year or budgetary window, and in this case there will be support for the investment in a premise model. Note there will normally be consulting services and training services associated with both models, which is a further expense that must be considered in order to have the solution fully configured and deployed, along with the user and administrator training that will help ensure the success of the solution.

As you review each of the ten areas, note that most organizations will see a pattern emerge that favors a cloud or premise deployment. This might not be what was expected in the beginning, so the process should be conducted with an objective and open mind-set.

If your organization is one that is truly split between cloud and premise across the ten areas, that is okay and simply means a more detailed analysis is required. This is time well spent and should ultimately lead you to an informed decision. What we have learned over the past ten years is that many organizations share common characteristics. But there is often a set of unique considerations that must not be overlooked and that keep us from taking a one-size-fits-all approach despite the thirty years of learning and experience we have in this market. I like to think of the flexibility of cloud and premise as ultimately a good thing for organizations today, as this provides a more complete and diverse opportunity to be successful.

> *The process of reviewing these ten areas and the discussions and debates it will spawn is a healthy one and will result in a more informed decision.*

And a more informed decision in support of what is likely to be a large corporate investment is a good thing for all. Key stakeholders and business experts should have a voice in this process and will help the organization to be better prepared regardless of which deployment model is selected in the end.

> *It is far better to contemplate and evaluate these points prior to lift-off, versus scrambling to find some alignment across the business when the deployment is in flight.*

Of course, you can add other points to this list of ten; this model should simply get the conversation started and provide a framework to build from, with the goal being an educated and thoughtful decision the organization can get behind and execute with confidence and clarity.

Note that some organizations will be making a deployment decision that is heavily weighted to one or two of these questions. For example, I have seen decisions made in favor of cloud strictly based on Year 1 costs. If a business simply must maximize money saved in the first year, this analysis will typically favor cloud as a natural function of the annual subscription costs versus the purchase of a perpetual license along with first-year maintenance costs.

Conversely, decisions have been made in favor of premise based largely on security and governance regulations. Some organizations require that IT applications and user or customer data are on premise and secured by local physical security procedures. As more organizations gain experience with SaaS applications, together with the continued improvements in SaaS availability and security, SaaS for Service Management is likely to continue to see growth in adoption by a wide range of Service Management teams.

> *Expect to see a continuing demand for both premise and cloud for IT Service Management far into the future.*

When making this decision, your organization should take the time to get all the current facts for both deployment models and take a thorough and self-critical look at the ten questions in this chapter. Of course there are many other good questions, and you should add any that can provide value to your decision-making process. I have suggested ten, as it is a manageable number and in most cases will allow the organization to explore each in some depth. This exploration will then yield an indicator for most organizations as to what the best overall model will be.

The goal is simply to select a deployment model that is best suited to the needs and nature of your organization. In doing so, the tool will assist you in achieving improved IT Service Management and, for some organizations, world-class performance. For additional thoughts on leveraging technology in a practical and successful way, see Chapter 21.

A CULTURE OF EXCELLENCE

Why a chapter on culture? Great question. The journey to world-class IT Service Management is about much more than tools, technology, processes, and best practices. Yes, of course these elements are important and certainly have a place. However, this journey—and it is a journey through and through—is very much about culture. To the extent that culture comes in at #1 in terms of what it takes to experience a journey that yields success and enables an organization to deliver services at a world-class level every day. And perhaps surprisingly and perhaps not, culture can be overlooked when businesses are mapping out a strategy to be successful in navigating the journey that lies ahead.

Note that we don't describe the journey as finished or completed. This is not a matter of crossing the finish line. That does not happen per se. While we do achieve new levels of excellence and pass important milestones over time, our journey is never complete. We strive to improve, sometimes with very small steps and sometimes with larger steps. Small or large, consistent and ongoing improvement is only possible with a culture that has the qualities and displays the behaviors that make the first step on the journey possible.

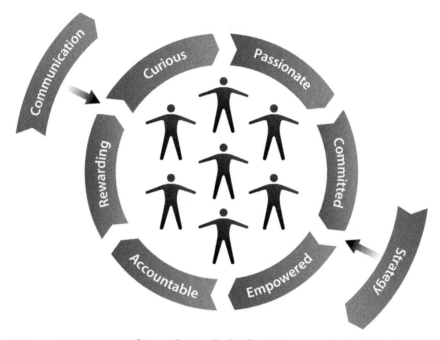

Figure 20.1 A Cultural Model That Generates Success

Successful and high-performing cultures share a number of traits. I have highlighted eight of these here, but there are, of course, others and variations of these same elements. I'm particularly fond of these and see most of them present in a world-class IT Service Management organization. Let's take a brief look at each.

Passionate

Passion is the fuel that makes many things possible. Passion creates energy and overcomes the inevitable obstacles that will appear throughout the journey. Passion can come from anywhere in the organization and is very contagious. Passion gives rise to confidence, a transformational quality that can make the impossible seem possible and changes the way we view everything. Passion also naturally creates a sense of deep caring that can in turn create focus, allowing us to see many things clearly that otherwise might be missed when viewed by a team that does not share the same sense of focus. Never underestimate the power of passion.

Committed

Be committed. Be completely committed every day. This must apply to executives and to management, as the lack of this support from the top and through every level of the organization will ultimately create problems. Challenges and issues are inevitable and will test the commitment of the organization. If the commitment is not strong, these challenges can result in delays, setbacks, and in the worst cases, a failed project. With strong commitment, the organization will rise to meet these challenges and in many cases will emerge from a challenging period all the stronger. Once committed to world-class IT Service Management, the organization takes on the mind-set of **doing whatever it takes** to find success. World-class teams show remarkable commitment.

Strategic

Define the right strategy, both for the business and for delivering great service. Then socialize this strategy and take care to ensure every team is in line with the strategy. No need to be perfect here; the strategy can evolve over time. The most common mistakes are not taking the time to define the strategy, or having the strategy and not achieving an understanding of it across the organization. People will react well to being part of this vital process, and with an understanding of the strategy, our teams will be in a position to make better decisions every day and to be an advocate for the strategy with those new employees or others who for some reason don't know or understand the strategy. With the context of the strategy, people can execute tactics better than when they are lacking visibility of the strategy.

Empowered

A culture of excellence is naturally equipped for world-class IT Service Management, and high-performing organizations will always include empowered employees. It is a simple but not an easy model. Identify the talented and knowledgeable people in the organization, assign them to key roles, and empower them to be successful. Mistakes are okay and ultimately lead to a more creative and aggressive business. This transformation to creative and aggressive is only possible when employees believe taking reasonable risks in order to get better is an accepted approach. Mistakes of commission are far better than complacency. An empowered workforce is also more willing to make decisions and to avoid the costly delays associated with waiting. In many ways, waiting is the greatest risk of all and common in cultures where employees are not empowered.

Accountable

Accountability balances empowerment. We can't have one without the other. High-performing individuals and teams welcome accountability. As with commitment, this starts with senior leadership and must be present at every level of the organization. Many desirable behaviors are born of accountability. This is a case where the benefits of accountability go far beyond this single word and idea. The best people demand and expect empowerment and then are prepared and willing to accept accountability. The essence of this relationship is very important because the results are clear—a stronger workforce and a stronger business. With this, we then will also see the added benefit of attracting and retaining the very best people who are drawn to this type of culture. Good begets good.

Rewarding

We all share an innate desire to be recognized. This is a deeply rooted and strong instinct. Recognition and reward go hand in hand and satisfy our emotional and practical needs. Take the time to reward the right behavior and the desired results. People will notice and quickly follow suit. This is a powerful model for which there is virtually no downside. The momentum created by recognition and reward can be remarkable, and this momentum first encourages and then creates the right behaviors, the right decision-making, and ultimately the right results. This in turn forges understanding and rapidly expanding expectations of excellence. Another value in this model is that even the small and simple rewards are powerful. In most cases it is not the size or the form of recognition that is appreciated by the people of an organization; it is simply the recognition itself.

Communicative

Tireless communication is a lifeblood of excellence. This is our organizational sensory system for good news, bad news, and all necessary information to keep performance every day on track. Many problems in business are created by simple misunderstandings that can be prevented with communication. Informal and frequent communication is easier than ever with voice, chat, social media, and email tools readily available. Informal and frequent communications are less costly to create and distribute and allow the organization to stay current, make better decisions, and make decisions more quickly. This series of actions will then result in better and faster service. As mentioned earlier, waiting is an organizational poison and the enemy of excellence. We want to work hard every day to prevent waiting and to prevent decisions which will ultimately result in apathy. In contrast, effective communication results in decisive action, an empowered workforce, no waiting, and broad and deep speed of execution across the organization.

Curious

Curiosity is a wonderful thing. This is a highly desirable trait in an organization and one that should be encouraged and cultivated. Curiosity leads to questions like Why and How, along with other questions that can lead to understanding and to finding a better way. We won't get better and we can't be great without curiosity. When we are curious we learn and we nurture growth and knowledge. Curiosity is a trait that can be modeled at virtually every level of the organization, and is another behavior that is highly contagious. It is a beautiful thing to watch curiosity spread through an organization and, along with it, the innovation and incremental improvements in virtually everything we do that will inevitably follow. Curiosity is also an engine for passion and energy, other traits that are key drivers of excellence.

> *You can see the striking similarities between cultural excellence and world-class IT Service Management.*

We can make the argument, preferably with a good bottle of wine, that they are one and the same. The one thing to remember is that in the pursuit of world-class service, a shift in culture must occur. Often it is large, but large will normally come in small steps. In recognizing that this strong force is needed and therefore highly desired, we can prepare for it from the beginning, which will in turn increase the chances of success that is only possible with the transformation of the culture. Now, I can't say what your shift will require, because every organization is different. What I can tell you is where to start. It begins with commitment.

From the CEO to every member of the IT organization and the Service Desk staff, an absolute commitment to the journey is the first step. With this simple beginning, each subsequent step will be a little bit easier and faster, and we are on the path to the success bred by delivering great service and creating happy customers.

CHAPTER 21

AN APPROACH TO LEVERAGE TECHNOLOGY

Today, world-class IT Service Management is more attainable than ever. A few key advancements in the past ten years have transformed how we deliver great service. These advancements include, in no particular order:

1. Maturity of IT best practices
2. The consumerization of IT
3. A broader community of experienced service management practitioners
4. Availability of more advanced technologies, including software applications well suited to IT Service Management

We have explored point #1 throughout the book with our Core 6 and World-Class 12 elements. And we took a closer look at the exciting consumerization of IT in Chapter 18.

Because virtually every Service Desk and IT Service

Management organization leverages one or more software applications, we will explore this topic to accelerate our journey to good, to great, and ultimately to world-class.

There are two primary phases, each to be managed successfully in order to leverage software applications fully:

1. Evaluation and selection of the right solution
2. Implementation and configuration

In this chapter I put forward a proven framework to guide your efforts in each phase. This structured approach will save you precious time and money while also reducing your risk.

✔ **Client Base**

✔ **Product Road Map**

✔ **Use Case Demo**

✔ **Support for Core 6 and World-Class 12**

✔ **Workflow Flexibility**

✔ **Service Catalog Adaptability**

✔ **Know the TCO**

✔ **Multi-Channel Support**

✔ **Business Terms**

Figure 21.1 Evaluation and Selection Criteria

Each of the following summaries are written from the standpoint of providing guidance to an organization in the process of evaluating and selecting the best-equipped software application and partner.

Client Base

Happy clients are a strong testament to the quality of a software tool and the business behind it. Request a list of client names, clients in the same market, and taking it a bit further, how many clients have been using the product for over five years. The standard IT Service Management application replacement cycle is four to five years, so a longer tenured client base says a lot. From the client base, speak with a few and ask pointed questions, not just the standard stuff. Ask about challenges faced during the implementation and how the vendor responded to the challenges to make things right.

Product Roadmap

The right software solution will be strong today and stronger in the future. What you are looking for is a partner that is investing to continue the evolution and improvement of the solution. It is not easy for a vendor to develop a good roadmap and to keep it alive and current, so don't expect many vendors to offer this up for your review. As such you should insist on seeing the roadmap, its contents, and the frequency of new releases. Persist with this request and you can learn a great deal from this review.

Use Case Demo

Every vendor can show a standard demo that looks great. You want to dig deeper. Drive the demo to a set of use cases that reflect key business processes in your organization— the key tasks your team performs every day in doing their job. I recommend five to ten good use cases as a manageable number, including a few that are particularly complex and challenging. Hold back two or three use cases that the vendor must build on the fly in a live demo. This will help separate the best solutions from the rest and will be a good indication of how configurable and adaptable the solution will be in day-to-day use. Watch carefully the process the vendor follows to build these on-the-fly scenarios and how much time is required. This will be very enlightening. Some vendors won't like it, but this process is all about identifying the best solution, and mixing things up with the vendor is in your best interest.

Support for Core 6 and World-Class 12 Processes

Your implementation of an IT Service Management solution will include some number of the processes outlined in the middle of this book. Most organizations are operating an average of four to six processes today, with a plan to add more processes in the future. Whatever your plan is, you should expect strong support of the Core 6, as most organizations will require most if not all of these six, and your journey to world-class IT Service Management will likely extend into some number of the additional six.

> *The key is knowing your areas of emphasis and exploring the capabilities the software solution can provide to meet your goals.*

At this stage it helps to have your own roadmap of processes and when you expect to go live with each. The software application can then be aligned with your timeline. If you happen to be one of the very few that are, or aspire to be, operating more processes than our World-Class 12, the same approach holds true: You will likely create a process design/model similar to what I have presented for the twelve showcased in this book, and your model(s) can then be used to broaden the evaluation to suit your needs.

Workflow Flexibility

Whether you are operating a single process, likely Incident Management, or the full set of the World-Class 12 and beyond, the workflow and automation capabilities of a software application are vital to success and yet sometimes overlooked. Surprising but true. It does make some sense when you consider that workflow is not normally addressed by the best-known IT best practice frameworks, and as a result it often remains in the background.

> *Service automation is, however, a key to success from a practical—what it really takes to make this all work—standpoint.*

In recognition of this reality, we gave the topic of service automation a chapter of its own. Chapter 16 should give you some good ideas of what to look for in your evaluation process, realizing that workflow must be powerful and at the same time easy to change, because your business will never stop changing, and the workflow model must be able to keep up.

Service Catalog Adaptability

The growing role of Service Catalog today places additional

emphasis on this capability. I identify it as a strategic element of the solution and not just another set of features. The star of Service Catalog is expected to rise in the future, so take the time to look closely during the evaluation. What we want to explore is general ease of use, ability to configure the user experience, ability to brand the catalog to your organization, number of out-of-box request templates, ease of adding a new request offering, ability to model cost, and the capability of the workflow model to support Service Catalog processes. Take this a bit further and give the ven dor an example of a new service offering; ask them to walk you through step by step, noting exactly what it takes to add this new request to the catalog. This process will reveal a lot.

Know the TCO

Too often the total cost of ownership (TCO) does not receive enough attention during the evaluation and selection phase. This is a mistake, because the TCO becomes a critical consideration over time and a key driver to the value equation for a solution. There are three important time bands to consider in the TCO:

1. Upfront costs to purchase the solution
2. Costs for implementation and deployment
3. Ongoing, recurring costs to operate

Make sure you request and receive a complete breakout of all three items. And although there are some differences inherent in SaaS (annual subscription contract) versus on premise (perpetual license + annual maintenance), both models should include training, system administration consulting services, and technical support. For item #3, I recommend a minimum of a three-year horizon, and five years is even better. Also, be sure to understand the normal timeline for implementation in item #2, with the vendor providing proof points for clients just like you.

Multi-Channel Support

The concept of multi-channel support was introduced in Chapter 16 (Service Automation) and shown in Figure 16.6. Most companies today are operating some version of this model, with a typical model being phone, email, and walk-up. However, we expect this model to expand in the future as demanded by a mobile workforce, improved technology, and the consumerization of IT. These forces will only grow, and any evaluation process for an IT Service Management solution should anticipate the expansion of multi-channel support. Incorporate a minimum of one use case for this model in the demo process. You should explore the number of channels supported by the vendor and plans to create more channels in the future. This is a good place to look for innovation—creative solutions or unique technologies not offered by other vendors.

Business Terms

This is a vital element, but another of our often overlooked items in the evaluation phase. Business terms can include pricing, terms and conditions, contracts and agreements. Traditionally, these documents are reviewed and pricing negotiated in the final steps of vendor selection. A more proactive approach is to request a preliminary review of contracts and agreements earlier in the process. In the case of a multi-year contract, it is important to understand all terms throughout the contract period. In the case of a single-year agreement, understand the renewal process and what might change. For example, will there be a price increase at the time of renewal for the new year? If so, what will that be? Is the vendor willing to define year-over-year increases on the price quote to avoid surprises? This will help reduce your risk in the future, and there are extensions of this theme that you can explore. For example, if you purchase more seats of the same product, what will the price be? The goal here is to avoid surprises and to reduce your exposure in the future.

> *Another benefit of addressing the business terms earlier in the process is that you will get an indication of the kind of partner the vendor will be.*

Is the vendor willing to work with you or will they be inflexible? Is the contract client-friendly or written in favor of the vendor? Is the vendor willing to offer some reasonable predictability in the future? You will likely have other points and questions to add to the discussion. Throughout this process you will develop a pretty good idea of how the vendor does business, which could cause you to reevaluate the overall grade or ranking of the vendor. When this review and negotiating happens at the very end of the vendor selection process and with only your preferred vendor, it is much more difficult to rewind the process and bring other vendors back in. I'm not suggesting that you have these discussions with a large group of vendors—that is just not practical. But it can be done with a smaller group of two or three vendors and help you identify the best vendor/partner for the future.

Implementation

As with evaluation and selection, we will put forward a proven framework to help guide the activities around the implementation of an IT Service Management software solution.

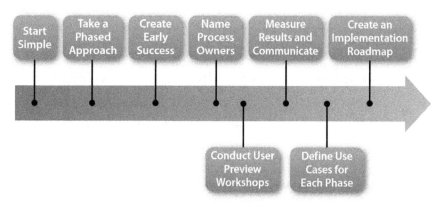

Figure 21.2 The Implementation Framework

Start Simple

The single greatest risk to the success of a software solution implementation is an overly ambitious plan that calls for unachievable deliverables against an unachievable timeline. Put another way: too much too soon. It is very important—no, it is vital—that you define reasonable and well-understood deliverables to start your project. This is not the time to tackle tough problems and sort out complexity.

If we frame this in terms of the twelve processes we have defined in the scope of the book, I recommend that organizations start with no more than three processes, and two is even better. For example, Incident and Service Catalog, or Incident and Problem are a couple of good combinations. If you already have a healthy Incident Management process in place, then you can look to add other processes. If not, Incident should be included in phase one for most organizations as a fundamental requirement for operating a strong Service Desk. You simply can't build a world-class IT Service Management operation without first implementing a strong Service Desk.

A few things to keep in mind as you are getting started:

 Build a Detailed Story Board or Flowchart for Every Process Before Undertaking That Step in the Project.

 Name a Process Owner/Expert to Work as an Advisor Throughout the Implementation of That Element.

 Create a Master Plan or Road Map for the Full Implementation. This Will Be Updated Many Times and That is OK.

 Phase I Must Be Designed to Virtually Assure Success Recognizing the Significance of this Early Success.

 Name a Communication Owner and Create a Communication Plan - Internal to the Project Team and Outbound to the Organization.

Figure 21.3 Getting A Good Start

Take a Phased Approach

Another enemy to the success of an implementation is a single, large, monolithic, and complex project timeline with a correspondingly large set of deliverables. The duration of these timelines is normally one to two years and will include the full set of IT Service Management processes, normally five to eight, to be implemented. This is done with the belief that there are efficiency and speed advantages inherent in this approach.

> *This is simply not the case, and many projects have failed in pursuit of this big bang approach.*

A single-phase project with a single timeline and single set of deliverables creates a high level of risk and normally results in slower progress and a high degree of rework. With this rework comes delays and wasted resource.

A multi-phase approach with several related sets of deliverables is a better model for success.

> *This approach will include natural checkpoints for feedback and the opportunity to make timeline and deliverable adjustments as needed.*

This could also be described as iterative and evolutionary. A typical model would include three to five phases, with each running three to six months depending on the resources available and the deliverables included in the phase. The cycle for each phase would look something like this:

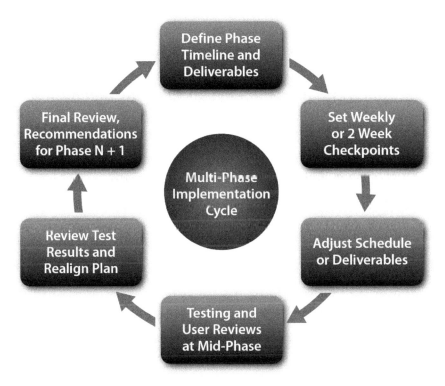

Figure 21.4 Phased Project Model

Create Early Success

From day one, it is important to manage expectations and to create, negotiate, and communicate a scope for Phase 1 that can be a success. There will be a lot of excitement around the project and a natural desire to be aggressive with the timeline and deliverables. This is understandable. But this is a time to be disciplined and thoughtful when creating the plan. That is not to say that we should be overly conservative and not make good use of company resources. What we require at this time is simple: a successful start.

> *So we must define an initial scope and take on processes that we are highly confident can be completed on schedule and on budget.*

In the context of our Core 6 processes, some combination of Incident, Service Catalog, and Problem Management is a good place to start. Three processes should be a maximum. Two would be better.

We take this measure approach to Phase 1 because much is at stake. If we fail to meet expectations and deliver what is required by the business, the project could be stalled, or worse yet, cancelled. This will rob the organization of the potential value associated with success. If we are successful with Phase 1, we have taken a big step toward making world-class IT Service Management a reality.

> *It is not an exaggeration to say that in many ways this first phase is the most important.*

So much becomes possible with a successful start.

The team earns recognition, credibility, and the trust of the organization. This in turn gives us improved access to budget and to the resources we need to deliver successful future phases. Our journey to world-class service delivery and world-class IT operations must begin with a great Phase 1.

One more thing: Take the time to communicate your success widely across the organization. Be proud of what you have accomplished. Have a Phase 1 success luncheon, or do a fun off-site activity with the team.

> **_It is important to celebrate success, large and small._**

Other people will notice and will want to be part of it.

Name Process Owners

As your team moves through the implementation process, many questions will arise, and it is important that these questions are answered quickly and accurately. Recognize that we are building a process design: If our design is not correct, it will at some point become clear there is a design flaw that needs to be corrected. That healing will take precious time and resources.

> **_And the later in the process any mistakes are detected, the more expensive it will be to correct._**

Note that I used the word _heal_ and not _fix_. This is the appropriate description, because what will be necessary is a process, not a single step or quick fix, to alleviate the anguish or pain the organization is experiencing. This is a reminder that every effort should be made to design and implement our processes correctly the first time. That goal is simple and one everybody would support, but it is not clear how we make that happen. In this section and in the next section, we will explore two tactics to reduce the risk of creating a poor process design.

Find the experts in your organization and get them involved early.

Name a process mentor or expert for each process who will be the go-to person for clarifications and to answer any questions that arise. These people are likely to jump at the chance to be part of the team, and can bring valuable experience and knowledge to the effort. Back to our risk issue around not getting it right the first time, the involvement of your experts will create a stronger cross-functional team and maximize the quality of process design, workflows, business rules, forms, and more. The process mentors can also help in creating good test cases, provide input to documentation and online help, and develop content for training tools and classes. While it is not possible to eliminate the risk of the costly rework, this approach greatly reduces that risk while spinning off lots of other benefits.

Conduct User Workshops

The traditional implementation process has little or no user involvement. This results in limited user visibility of the solution prior to reaching major deliverables, and this approach increased risk and often led to misunderstand-ings and schedule delays.

> ***A better approach is to design user activ-ity into the process with frequent, informal workshops.***

These workshops are intended to increase user visibility, to catch any misinterpretation of requirements early, to have an open discussion on key points, and to make mid-course corrections as needed. These workshops can be short and simple and provide a snapshot of the process currently be-ing configured—resulting in either a confirmation that we are on the right track or an opportunity to make changes as needed before working further into the process, where changes become harder and harder to make.

> ***This model is good for everybody. The us-ers appreciate the sneak preview, and the project team gets the best possible and very real feedback.***

The system users are ultimately customers who will be a judge of success. It is important to keep the reviews in-formal and focused. This can be done over lunch, or bring in pizza at the end of the day and make it a fun thing. The project team need not prepare documents or scripts for the meeting and just show real product, product prototypes, or wireframes. For example, a workshop could show an exam-ple of the Create incident form or the Incident Management workflow model. Another example would be the Service

Catalog interface and the initial set of service requests in the catalog.

> ### *The users won't be shy—you will hear what is good, what is bad, and ideas on how to make it better.*

This is exactly what we are looking for and an hour well spent.

Measure Results and Communicate

At the beginning of each phase, you must define what success looks like and how it will be measured. If this is not clear, there might be a problem with the scope and deliverables for that phase. Now is the time to get this sorted out, not at the end of the phase. It will only get harder with the passing of time. The definition of success aligns the team and creates common goals.

> ### *This also calls to our attention that success must be measurable and not subjective or left to interpretation.*

This has another benefit in that it will provide the information we use to communicate back to the organization the good news on the progress we are making. An example of this template follows; remember to keep it simple.

Phase #: [   ]

Completion Date: [   ]

Goal 1: [   ]

Goal 2: [   ]

Goal 3: [   ]

Success Metric 1: [   ]

Success Metric 2: [   ]

Success Metric 3: [   ]

Comments: [   ]

Figure 21.5 Success Criteria

It's a good practice to be proactive in creating a report card and communicating how the project is performing. If a "metric void" exists, that is not a good thing. It will likely be filled by another team as a natural reaction, and the result won't be as meaningful as what the primary team can generate. Move quickly to create the measurements and share them with the organization. If there are problems, including a failure to meet one or more of the success metrics, keep a policy of complete transparency and communicate any problems and what is being done to address the issue to prevent any recurrence.

Define Use Cases For Each Phase

Each implementation phase will include a mix of technical- and business-related activities. An effective tool to bring the activities together and to create a common framework that connects the day-to-day activities of the phase to the ultimate success of the project is the creation of a set of use cases. The use cases should follow a set of guidelines to bring the necessary guidance and value to the business.

 Should Reflect Key Business Processes

 Should Be Well Understood and Described by a Detailed Storyboard

 Should Represent High Volume or the Most Time Consuming Tasks

 Should Be Related to the Primary Goals of the Phase

 Should Include a Definable Set of Success Criteria

Figure 21.6 Guidelines for Use Cases

The use cases serve many purposes. The right use cases will be well understood by the users or customers and help keep them involved in the implementation process. The use cases will also provide a good guide for testing activities to validate the configuration of the application and to ensure any business rules or workflows are providing the correct results. Another benefit of the use case is the support it provides to the training program. The use cases eliminate any need to translate application capabilities into a combination of functions and menus and forms that make sense to the intended user. This translation is already done by the use case; it should reflect a real day in the life of the user and help the user to perform their job better and faster. The number of use cases should be moderate and manageable—too few and we don't get adequate coverage, and too many slows the process down and can be redundant. We are looking for moderation.

Create An Implementation Roadmap

Before finalizing a plan for Phase 1 or any subsequent phase, it is important to create an implementation roadmap. This roadmap exercise is valuable as it confirms the key goals of the implementation, general timeframe, and strategic assumptions. It can also provide a targeted completion date and some definition of the processes to be included in the scope of the complete project. With this context, we can then provide Phase 1 and a tentative plan for Phase 2 and beyond. Staying true to the model shown in Figure 21.4, we then execute the implementation cycle for Phase 1 based on the performance, testing, and reviews in Phase 1.

At the end of each phase, in addition to updating the plan for the next phase, we also turn a critical eye to the implementation roadmap. The lessons learned from each phase—and we will certainly learn a lot from each phase—will improve both the more tactical plan for the next phase and the more strategic plan held by the roadmap. This is a good balance; we are constantly validating the execution of a phase with the context provided by the roadmap.

> **This is a world-class behavior, and we should not accept any shortcuts.**

Any shortcut would bypass the creation of the roadmap prior to Phase 1, and process lapses may allow the roadmap to become outdated and therefore of little value during the execution of each phase.

In addition to the context and validation the roadmap provides in guiding our execution of each phase, it is very helpful when communicating with management, stakeholders, process owners, and across the organization. The roadmap makes the direction clear—where we are today and where we are going.

> **The roadmap should be easy to understand and attract lots of attention, which, of course, is a good thing.**

This creates awareness, then understanding, and finally alignment and assistance.

Technology has a place in the delivery of world-class service, but it is important to understand what it can and cannot do. In combination with a motivated workforce, a healthy culture, and a reasonably phased implementation plan,

> *technology is a force multiplier that can make the vision of world- class IT Service Management a reality.*

However, technology can't save a culture that is not committed to a high standard or a fundamentally flawed implementation plan. If your organization has focused on cultural readiness, selected the right set of processes from the twelve we have reviewed throughout the book, and followed the recommendations outlined here for tool selection and implementation, you are well positioned to be successful and transform your business while elevating IT Service Management to the highest standard. This is within your reach.

THE FUTURE OF IT SERVICE MANAGEMENT

The future of IT Service Management is bright, perhaps brighter than ever. Never in our rich history of the thirty years since the birth of the Help Desk have we seen such a transformation in our craft. The transformation today has been addressed in Chapter 6 on Service Catalog, Chapter 16 on Service Automation, Chapter 17 on Enterprise Service Management, and Chapter 18 on the Consumerization of IT Service Management. Beyond the continued improvements in our practices related to the World-Class 12 processes, these four areas are reshaping IT today and fundamentally redefining the relationship of IT with the broader business.

Even with this remarkable progress we have seen in IT Service Management over the past decade, there is evidence that we are just getting started.

*In this final chapter we turn our eyes to
the future and what is likely to be a set of
themes and forces that set the course of IT
and the practice of Service Management,
along with the operation of the Service
Desk, over the next decade and beyond.*

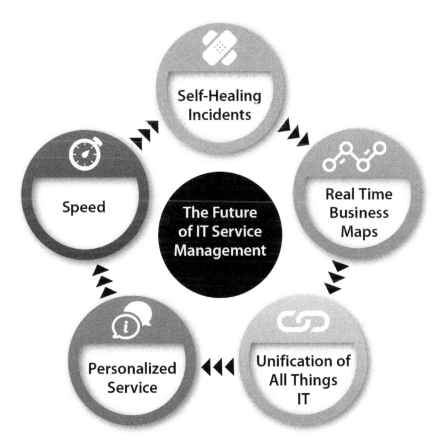

Figure 22.1 A Model for the Future of IT

I expect to see a quantum leap forward in the most fundamental of processes, Incident Management, in the years
ahead. The combination of our great experience with

managing tickets and incidents over the past thirty-plus years, together with improved technology and a new class of algorithms, has put us at the threshold of a completely new paradigm for managing incidents. **Self-healing incidents** will identify a potential issue, evaluate the context, assess the facts available, analyze the risk of failure, model the likely outcome, cross-reference this predictive outcome with known history, and then take corrective action—all in a matter of milliseconds and before any customer or analyst is aware of or sees any symptom of an incident. This advanced model with self-healing includes the majority of what would have been a traditional incident before any human action is required. Although this scenario is not common today, it is now within our reach. Expect to see this capability deployed more widely over the next five to ten years. Embracing new capabilities and the technologies that enable them is not an easy transition, so this won't happen quickly. But the powerful pull of these benefits will not be denied.

There is no better way to communicate a great deal of information quickly and in a manner that is easily understood than with a good graphical image. A benefit of world-class IT Service Management is a new understanding of the relationships between services, infrastructure assets, and the customers who consume these services. The objects and actions associated with incidents, problems, changes, and releases then intersect and influence the primary relationship of service/asset/customer. A **real-time business map** would provide a dynamic view of the complete IT estate, including every service that is currently in-flight, the service components and assets that are being utilized by each of these services, and the customers who are consuming them. This graphical map is updated by a rapid pulse from the business and shows a true, real-time view of all IT activities and actions. Think of the combination of an air traffic control radar at a busy airport combined with a New York subway schedule board. This real-time business map would become the primary tool used by analysts, IT management, and executive leadership to quickly assess the state of the organization, all in real time with accurate information.

Traditionally we think of services, infrastructure, and assets, along with IT security, as three somewhat distinct and separate organizations, sets of tools, teams of people, and processes. There are many good reasons why this was the case historically, but this model is beginning to change. And I expect this change to accelerate.

What will occur is a **true unification of all things IT**—infrastructure, service delivery, and the security of all service components and corporate assets.

This unification will reflect that these three elements are inextricably linked in achieving a world-class model of service delivery driven by a highly productive and secure business infrastructure. This is in part due to our growing recognition that the segregation of these elements in the past was due to limitations in tools and processes, and not truly the most powerful model for the organization. We can think of the past model as a compensation for what was lacking in the way of tools and immature processes.

Today we awake to a different landscape on both counts. The unification of IT that lies ahead has many benefits, including:

1. The elimination of unnecessary integrations and handoffs
2. Better communications
3. A significant improvement in resource utilization
4. A more empowered team
5. Faster response times
6. Dramatically improved organizational velocity

This word *velocity* is much used and sometimes abused, but I do like the term and use it here to mean that everything happens faster. And I mean *everything,* because what occurs is a chain reaction of one element of the business moving faster, which then enables the next to move faster, then the next, and so it goes. This is limitless and in many cases born of this unification.

The history of IT and the Service Desk was very much about efficiency and the reduction of costs. This was perfectly appropriate for the era and what the business needed at the time, and for the birth and growth of the Help Desk, then giving way to the Service Desk. Today, the rules and needs of our organization are in flux. Where in the past our focus on efficiency and cost did not preclude personalized service per se, it certainly did not encourage it, as it was not clear how all of these objectives could be accomplished at the same time. With no disruptive influence driving a fresh look at priorities, IT carried on, seeking incremental improvements in efficiencies and cost reductions. We often heard "do more with less" or "do more with the same"—resources and budgets, that is.

In the next decade, we will turn this model on its head, and personalized service will become mandatory for world-class IT Service Management. Efficiency gains and cost management won't get us there. Yes, these two factors are important but not world-class in and of themselves. The journey to world-class simply won't be successful without a strategy to deliver **highly personalized services or products each and every time** and to adapt quickly when those personal needs change as they always do. This is not easy and many organizations will not be able to conquer this challenge. Perhaps even most won't. But make no mistake, the market leaders of the future will, with the source of this shift being in IT and then propagating this model across the full organization. The seed of world-class can be found in IT and at the Service Desk.

If you have read more than a page or two of this book, you have likely come across a reference to the value of speed. Speed has been part of our discussion on many fronts—the Consumerization of IT Service Management in Chapter 18, for example, as well as Service Automation in Chapter 16—because speed is inseparable from these topics as well as the overall objective of world-class performance. I raise the point of speed here one final time because its importance continues to climb the list of priorities for IT, IT Service Management, and the entire organization. Some themes are important, and a few can fundamentally change the business and create a competitive advantage and a growing group of thrilled customers. **Raw speed is one of these special**

themes and will be one of the strategic investments that shape the next ten years and beyond. There are few downsides to speed in the context of Service Management and virtually unlimited upside. With a constant level of service quality and cost, what customer is not excited about getting what they need, and getting it faster? In any maturing market, products and services become more alike and increasingly commoditized. Then, speed changes everything.

These five agents of change are certainly not the only factors that will shape the next ten to twenty years of IT and IT Service Management. I have selected these as a sample of what exactly will emerge as driving this transformation of IT today and are likely to prove of lasting value and as such carry forward for the next ten years and beyond.

While my experiences with leading businesses have resulted in a personal view of what is to come, your view may very well be different. Ultimately we will discover the answers together as we embrace and enjoy the surprises and the learning that only the future can bring.

FINAL THOUGHTS

Each one of us is fortunate to be part of the exciting transformation of IT and Service Management that surrounds us today. We are, together, being swept forward by the powerful market forces that surround us, and at the same time, we are integral to creating and sustaining these forces.

Regardless of the nature of your organization or the size of your business, I hope that from the many strategies, models, concepts, and tips I have presented in the preceding pages, you can take a few ideas that can help move your organization forward on this fantastic journey to world-class IT Service Management.

If you are one of those organizations already operating at a world-class level, then you understand we never stop searching for ways to improve. With this sustaining spirit and curiosity, my hope is that you will also find something in the book, even something subtle or small, that will help you get just a little better. Perhaps take a fresh look at something that was taken to be good enough. Remember, the small steps can, over time, be more important and create more value than those big leaps we take from time to time.

I implore you to never underestimate the impact that you as an individual and as a member of a team can have on your organization and all the people around you. This includes your management, as well as IT and corporate leadership. Your influence is virtually boundless. Role modeling can occur in many forms and take any direction. **Bring a passion to your role every day and a joy that springs from the enthusiastic pursuit of world-class in everything you do.**

Many things in business we simply can't control, and the cycle of business will inevitably bring ups and downs, successes and challenges, wins and losses. Your sense of optimism and confidence in yourself and in the people around you is something you fully control and can bring to every task, call, and meeting. This attitude also serves as the energy that will fuel the pursuit of lifting your organization to the next level.

Passion and optimism are remarkably contagious and can spread through a small team or a large enterprise with staggering speed. Be the catalyst of this action, and you will be amazed at the good things that start to happen. Never think for a moment that you can't or that you shouldn't. You can and you should!

Keep the faith, my friends. I look forward to hearing your stories when our paths cross.

Kevin

REFERENCES

1. The Help Desk Handbook, Ron Muns, Help Desk Institute, Copyright 1993.
2. The Visible Ops Handbook, Kevin Behr, Gene Kim and George Spafford, IT Process Institute Inc., Copyright 2004.
3. Executive's Guide to IT Governance, Robert W. Moeller, John Wiley & Sons Inc., Copyright 2013.
4. Manager's Guide to Compliance, Anthony Tarantino, John Wiley & Sons Inc., Copyright 2006.
5. ITIL For Dummies, Peter Farenden, John Wiley & Sons, Copyright 2012.
6. Foundations of ITIL V3, Jan van Bon, Van Haren Publishing, Copyright 2009.
7. Running An Effective Help Desk, Barbara Czegel, John Wiley & Sons Inc., Copyright 1998.
8. IT Governance, Peter Weill and Jeanne W. Ross, Harvard Business Review Press, Copyright 2004.

INDEX

Figures are indicated by "f" following the page number.

NOTES

NOTES

NOTES

NOTES

NOTES

_____
_____
_____
_____
_____
_____
_____
_____
_____
_____
_____
_____
_____
_____
_____
_____
_____
_____
_____
_____
_____
_____

NOTES

NOTES

NOTES

NOTES

NOTES

_____
_____
_____
_____
_____
_____
_____
_____
_____
_____
_____
_____
_____
_____
_____
_____
_____
_____
_____
_____
_____

NOTES

NOTES

NOTES

NOTES

NOTES

_____

_____

_____

_____

_____

_____

_____

_____

_____

_____

_____

_____

_____

_____

_____

_____

_____

_____

_____

_____

_____

_____

NOTES

_____
_____
_____
_____
_____
_____
_____
_____
_____
_____
_____
_____
_____
_____
_____
_____
_____
_____
_____
_____
_____
_____
_____
_____

NOTES

NOTES

NOTES

NOTES

NOTES

NOTES

NOTES

CPSIA information can be obtained
at www.ICGtesting.com
Printed in the USA
LVHW081327150219
607692LV00018B/159/P